THE

HOUSE CHURCH

MOVEMENT

Which Direction Will It Take ?

THE

HOUSE CHURCH

MOVEMENT

by

TOM BEGIER

TIM RICHEY

NICK VASILIADES

FRANK VIOLA

The House Church Movement
Which Direction Will It Take?

Copyright
MMI
by
SEEDSOWERS
Publishing House

Printed in
the United States of America

Published by
SEEDSOWERS
Christian Books Publishing House
P.O. Box 3317
Jacksonville, FL 32206
(800) 228-2665

See our exciting website at:
www.SeedSowers.com

Library of Congress Cataloging-In-Publication Data

ISBN 0-940232-75-8
1. Religious
2. Non-Fiction

Publisher's Note

The men who wrote this book have chosen not to identify which chapters each man wrote, preferring the book to speak with one voice.

DEDICATION:

To every Christian whose heart beats
for a dramatic change in all existing
church practices

ACKNOWLEDGEMENT

We extend our grateful thanks to Caroline Scott who retyped our manuscripts so many times the manuscript reached a mile high! And we thank Helen Edwards for extending to us her genius in the hundreds of hours she spent in editing and re-editing this book.

On the following page is a letter written by a man who recorded his reaction to having visited a house church . . . to be exact he visited one of the *radical* house churches

A LETTER SENT TO THE CHURCH IN MINNEAPOLIS BY A VISITOR

Last summer I met some Christians at a park in Onamia. They were really unusual. Every one of them, all ages, had so much fun with each other that I didn't feel like I was with a group of Christians but rather, a family.

Whenever I have been with a group of Christians before, for even a few minutes, I could always tell who was the leader, and who were the "spiritual" ones, etc. But with these people I couldn't tell them apart, as to who were the mature Christians, who were new Christians, who were involved in Christian work, who were the "inner group." And I could go on and on.

After the picnic I didn't see them for a few months. When I met them again we had a great time.

Then I went to Minneapolis and met with them in one of their meetings. They have really unusual meetings. Not everyone comes in with a Bible under his arm. No one opens their meetings in prayer; nonetheless, by the time the meeting ends, there will have been more prayer than you would hear in traditional meetings. No one takes the leadership. They don't have a time of prayer requests. They don't even talk about their problems or needs. They don't have Bible studies about their doctrines or the "right way to do things." They spend no time talking about their giftings or where they feel they fit in the Body.

It's difficult to figure out why they get together, other than simply Jesus, since there is no expression of their individual interests. They meet in someone's house. When they sing they don't sit around and sing like a group of individuals. They stand really close, as if they are bunching themselves into a tight group. They have their arms around each other and sing like they are one person singing to their Lord. The songs they sing are only about Jesus. They don't sing about their victory, their beliefs, the things they do for the Lord, the coming of the Lord, etc. They only sing songs about Jesus! Some of their songs they have written themselves. While they are singing someone will shout or someone will whisper a statement of their love for their Lord, or something about who He is to them. While singing they often make statements about His greatness or the greatness of all that He has done through Calvary, or the wonderful expressions of His love. It's as if they are more in love with Him than anything else in their lives.

(I have noticed that sometimes they also have pretty empty meetings, just like everyone else!)

They are very unorganized. They don't have a pastor or elders. They don't even have a doctrinal statement as a group. They don't have a name.

They call themselves a church but they don't act like any church I have ever been to. I didn't know that it was even possible to have a church with no pastor, elders or leader, but they have been meeting for three years! They told me that some have come and gone because they didn't understand or feel comfortable with their freedom. I can believe it.

No one talks about what they do for Him. They are only interested in Him. When they talk about Him they talk like He is a real person and not someone their doctrine is built around. They don't talk about the things He does for them but just Him. They don't give testimonies about their past. They are very interested in each other but could care less about each other's past.

You would think that their only benefit in being Christians is getting to know Him. They don't give testimonies about the healings or miraculous ways that God has provided for them. They don't give testimonies about the victory in their lives. It's as if any victory in their lives isn't worth noticing but He is worth noticing and any victory they have is His victory and not theirs anyway. They don't talk about how others should be like them. They talk about Him. They don't even talk down about others who are not like them.

They don't talk about how Christians should be gracious to each other, but they have an atmosphere of grace about them that is hard to put into words. They don't get excited about anything that they do. But when they talk about their Lord there is kind of a twinkle in their eyes. They have no expectations of how someone should act (and some act pretty silly sometimes). I hope that I haven't made them sound extremely "spiritual" because they are the most non-religious group of Christians I have ever met. And yet they know the Lord in a way that I haven't seen before either.

They just seem to be people who love to be around each other.

Their personalities are such a variety that if it were not for the Lord I'm sure they wouldn't even care to know each other. They don't even use religious terminology. (They don't talk like the Christians I have known.) They don't get on each others case because someone isn't doing something "right." In all these months of being with them I have never heard "you should" either stated or implied. They joke with each other and do a lot of laughing. I have known individuals in churches who got along really well and did a few things together, but these people *all* do things together. They just seem to enjoy each other. It's weird how they obviously love each other dearly and love the Lord dearly and yet they don't show it in ways that I'm used to.

They don't overtly tell each other about their love for each other; still, it is so obvious that it doesn't need to be said.

They say they are not interested in getting together to develop relationships, yet they are closer to each other than most believers I know. It's as if they are not trying to accomplish anything and yet they have everything that I have always heard Christians talk about wanting.

As to doctrine, I don't know what they each believe. And they don't ask me about mine! That I love Jesus and that I am in Him is all that they are interested in.

No one gets preferential treatment; yet everyone gets preferential treatment! I have never known such non-special people and yet there is something that gives them a specialness.

I know I sound like I'm rambling. But it is hard to describe something I've never seen before.

What is Meant by House Churches

Many of the large institutional churches have meetings in homes. *That* is *not* what this book is about.

There are little groups all over America who meet in houses but are not taking "house church" all that seriously. These folks are *not* going to turn the world upside down. Nor are their workers and leaders.

Such a version of house church is not what this book is about.

This book is about the house church becoming a revolutionary force so endued that it will turn church history upside down. It is about becoming a force as great or greater than the Reformation of the 1500's.

PART I

The House Churches . . .
What Are Your Choices?

1

One of These Is
Not Like the Other

Two men, John and Henry, step out of
their respective houses. Both men belong to
the house church movement. Both are on
their way to a meeting. One gets into a car,
the other walks across the street. But the two
men, going to different meetings, will have
experiences that are poles apart.

John drives across town to his meeting.
Arriving at a nice suburban neighborhood, he
goes in and sits down in a living room filled
with about twenty middle-class Americans.
He finds himself in a rather stoic atmosphere,
one of quietness and reverence.

When everyone has arrived, the meeting starts with a "word of prayer." Usually
the man or woman with the strongest personality begins to lead the meeting. Then come

three or four prayers. In meetings like John's, someone may speak in tongues *or* someone reads from the Scriptures, depending on which kind of group it is. A half-dozen songs are sung. Then comes Bible study.

The brother who shares from the Bible is usually *the* one person who *always* shares in every meeting. He leads. Sometimes he dominates!

A few years ago John attended a traditional church. Now he prefers the atmosphere and camaraderie of meeting in a living room with a few brothers and sisters. What he does not realize is, just as he was once there for the pastor's purpose, he is now there for the purposes of someone with a strong personality. And that person *needs* to lead . . . and to dominate. In so doing, such leaders can have their egos satisfied and their dreams fulfilled.

For John, the difference between the organized church and his house church is *nil*. After all, the modern-day pastor is fulfilling his dream wish, and so also is the house church leader. John left the traditional church and moved into a living room, yet he is still just a pawn in the hand of a leader-bent individual.

This book is written by men who are in no way satisfied with either the institutional church meetings or those of most house churches.

To that point let us look at Henry.

Henry is also on his way to a meeting. But he doesn't get in a car. *He walks across the street.*

John ended up in a living room because he was interested in church renewal. Henry was never looking for *church renewal.* He and others came together because they were madly, passionately after *Jesus Christ.*

Henry lives in the midst of a community of believers who are *not* "meeting-centered." They do not drive to one another's homes; they live within a block or two of one another. They spend their lives near one another. Furthermore they are part of a revolution. A radical revolution.

John does not experience what Henry experiences when he opens the door and enters a living room. Henry will not walk into a quiet, stoic, reserved room. Henry will walk into the benign chaos of *church life.* He will walk into a room where all the brothers and sisters are talking. Oddly enough, the meeting has already begun, although it may look like it has not! In fact, this meeting began *months* ago. Preparation for this meeting has been in the process for a long time. The meeting itself did not begin in that living room. It began on the street outside the house. In yet another way, the *real* beginning of this meeting started in early morning gatherings throughout the neighborhood, in groups of two's or three's.

Henry is a part of an *organic* experience of church life. John has no idea what that means, nor even that such things exist. He and his friends have settled for the *traditional* "church in the home." When Henry enters that living room, he may be greeted with "Hello, holy one!" Or maybe he will just be hugged. Henry responds in kind. Very soon thereafter—just about at the announced time for meeting—everyone moves to the middle of the room. They begin singing—singing mostly songs *they* have written! These are songs which have come out of their life with Christ and with one another.

There is no leadership-bent person controlling this meeting. There is no lone person dominating the direction of the meeting. No one particular person starts this meeting. No one particular person will end it! The meeting is started, directed, redirected, stopped, started again, up a hill, down a hill, through the eternals, out of the eternals . . . *all* by the brothers and sisters in the meeting.

No one person leads, yet the dynamic of the meeting never ebbs.

This meeting is not led by one who is trying to fulfill his ego or dream wish. This meeting is led by God's people, and by the Lord Himself. This meeting has no head except Jesus Christ. Yet everything flows. And everything makes sense. Nonetheless, there is always a sense of surprise as the meeting develops!!

There is much singing, much laughter, much testifying of the Lord and His riches— much testifying of the Lord *and* His *house*. All that is done by *all* the brothers and sisters in that room. Nor is it stilted nor does it smell of being organized. The meeting is a study in the organic nature of the *ekklesia*. To put it another way: Chances are, you've not seen or been in a meeting like this. Chances are neither have generations of Christians before you.

The situation John finds himself in did not "just happen." The situation Henry finds himself in did not "just happen." With purpose and forethought, both of these totally different kinds of meetings came into existence. The problem with John's situation is that the man who leads the group *created* that rather boring meeting.

The group of which Henry is part was planted by a man, too. But he is not in that meeting. Probably no one knows where he is. This man *in absentia* might be characterized by some as a wandering madman—a man possessed with Jesus Christ and with seeing His house return to this earth again . . . a man burning to see God's people walk in freedom, the freedom which is their birthright . . . a man determined to see God's people free of legalism . . . *and* God's people free to be in charge of their own gatherings . . . a man who settles for nothing less than God's people making their decisions, God's people reclaiming the ekklesia . . . and God's house belonging to God and His people rather than to a minister or a leader-bent individual. This very absent man has raised up an ekklesia that is given back to the Lord and to the Lord's people. He is a man who leaves—does not stay. A man who is not a local fixture.

Or, as previously stated . . . a revolutionist!!

When John leaves his house church meeting, he says a few good-byes, gets in his car and drives back across town to his house. He will probably have no contact with these people again until next week.

John lives a Christian life that is meeting-centered.

The meeting that Henry is in? It looks like a cross between an American birthday party, Monday night football (and maybe like it is when your team wins the Superbowl). Or it can express itself in a dozen different ways, or more!! It is an American expression. A free-flowing get-together of God's people, passionately going after Christ. *This* is church! The other? It is a drag.

When Henry leaves the meeting, he will head back across the street to his house with his arms around two or three brothers. As the men separate, they will call out salutations. When will they see one another again? *Not next week!* They will see one another tomorrow morning at 6 am . . . before the Lord.

John's meetings were set in motion for church renewal. The gathering which Henry is part of was set in motion for far more radical reasons: for a passionate pursuit of Jesus Christ being utmost in mind.

John goes to meetings. Henry is experiencing a way of life.

The meetings these two men go to are worlds apart. One draws strength from an ideal and a formula. The other draws its strength from a living vision *and* from other realms. The two meetings have origins that are worlds apart. Each has its origin coming from completely different mindsets.

Dear reader, if you are tired of sitting and listening, tired of stoic, reverent, regulated meetings, please know that this other world *does* exist. Your Lord is out there, living and breathing, on the streets of America. Will you know Him? That is, are you desperate enough to pursue Him?

If the answer is yes, I look forward to the possibility that I might one day meet you.

2

Only for the Desperate

The foundation of the house church movement is being laid even *now*. What kind of foundation is emerging? The answer is frightening.

Throughout all church history the great works of God were born in blazing fire and in explosions of revelation. Counterwise, most of the house church movement is theological, scholarly, academic, or, at best, shallow and anemic.

To illustrate what is abroad in the land, what is supposed to be new, great and deep, consider this: four-day conferences with fifteen speakers—most of them educators and seminarians. Or, a three-day conference on how *you* can have a house church. Or, worse, a one-day seminar on how to be a church planter, with a certificate given out at the end of the day certifying that *you* are qualified to be a church planter (or maybe even an apostle). This all speaks to the shallowness of most of the house church movement.

Contrast that to John Wesley, of the 1700's, throwing all Britain on its ear. Or frontier Baptists—on horseback—in burning heat and bitter cold, covering the entire American southlands. Fire was in their bones. Not to mention those witnesses to Christ in dark ages, such as the Anabaptists, Waldensians, and Plymouth Brethren, who turned church history in its course.

Many of God's people want a radical assault, an *extreme* approach, an earth-shaking new dimension in the practice of church. However, most of the house church movement is a yawn. It is, at best, a thing heavily layered with lectures by theoretical men.

Where is a dynamic of single mindedness? Where is that driving desperation of holy men seeking a new unheard-of approach to church? Not fads or gimmicks, but literally a laying aside of all present practices. An assault on unexplored heights as men claw their way into a new testimony of what *church* really is.

There are desperate people out there. Maybe you are one. Believers who will be satisfied with nothing less—things which bear no resemblance to anything which exists today. Church as it has never been seen, not in a thousand years.

Superficial methods in this divine matter of building will *not* do. (Those of us who penned this book are among those who have committed our lives to a new, revolutionary expression of church life.)

You can tell that something is terribly wrong when you see groups with shallow goals start up every week and shortly thereafter disappear, never to be heard of again. These are house churches built on sand. When the house church falls, no tears are shed. These groups are born on the wings of fluffy dreams, and no one either cares or notices when they vanish.

The foundation of anything truly new in Christendom must be radical, daring, and unprecedented. And that new work rocks the boat, drawing unprovoked controversy.

Thank God, in this generation, as in all generations, there are a few willing hearts ready to live for, to shed their blood for, and to die for . . . a white-hot, unique expression of the Christian faith. Such men and women are always marked by certain characteristics. They are *unwilling* to *quit*, no matter the circumstances! Nor the failure. Nor opposition. Obsessed—not with a theory—but with a revelation from God. A revelation that flows red hot in their blood stream. Men impelled! Unstoppable men. Men who not only have a revelation of God, but depth, *depth in Christ*! Men who are building a foundation that is itself ablaze with the fire and fury of God. Men who deliberately set out to build . . . that is, to lay a foundation which will last, not for a year or a decade, but a foundation built to last a thousand years.

Failure, set-back, and the fact the whole thing is impossible do not figure into the equation!

Are there such men to be found in the present house church movement?

Let's see.

In England? In general, the house church movement is already old and settled—scholarly, theoretical. Shallow beyond explaining. Elders rule. People sit and listen . . . to endless reams of messages. Further, those dear people get rained on with the doctrine of *authority* and *submission*. Legalism is three feet deep. Then there is the version of house churches where it is a tea and crumpets fellowship. This kind of house church has no purpose other than inane fellowship.

In Australia? Dominated by domination. Elders, theoreticians, hide-bound with Scripture verses, and—as always—a sit-and-listen laymanship.

New Zealand? The same.

In the United States, the very tiny house church movement is scholarly, legalistic and/or shallow as only we Americans are able to be.

What is the core need of the house church movement? Men and women bent on changing the status quo.

Are there such firebrands anywhere out there in the house church movement? Out of hundreds of frontline leaders and thousands of quickly-ordained dictators *called* elders, there may be a few, if you count the entire world. But you can number these men of fury on two hands—maybe *one*.

Go find them! When you do, follow them. They will lead you not into mild-mannered meetings where relationship and fellowship are held up as the end of all good. These men will, rather, lead you into a revolutionary, earth-shaking expression of community. Or, to say it another way: into a whole new venue of *church*. Into church which is radical, revolutionary, and extreme!

Find them. Follow them. Give them a little time and they will then set you free from following them . . . to *corporately* follow Christ. (Yes, they will come around again from time to time to help you, but that will be in order to move you back to focus on the centrality of Christ rather than to continue being your leader.)

These men burn with a revelation of Christ. They are there to remove, end and annihilate clergyism, hyper-elders, and dictatorship. These men release God's people to function. These men exist to give the church back to its *true* owners: (1) Christ and (2) *all* God's people. Such men are revolutionists of the highest order.

Dare God's people engage in such an enterprise? Most believe such days belong to men and women of bygone days. Not so. This is an age for revolutionary living . . . bolder than anything which came about "in bygone days."

3

Those Who Came Before

If you are considering becoming part of the radical expression of the house church, it would be the better part of wisdom to learn what has happened in centuries past. We encourage you to do many things. One is to learn the story of the dear radicals of the past. They have raised a standard for all of us. Learn everything that can be learned about those who have, for the last 1800 years, set out on that unique journey of returning to first principles. I strongly suggest you read of those who came before you.

Until those books are published, I recommend that you read *The Torch of the Testimony* or *Lost Heritage*. Learn the past story of Christians who stepped out of the institutionalized way of doing things.

Even while I pen these words, some of the authors of this book are writing new books on the history of Christian groups of the last 1800 years who stepped out of institutional Christianity.

Learn the story of those who, for 1800 years, have fought and died to return to the original revelation of the first century. What caused these people to risk everything? What caused them to move in a direction that was against the accepted practices of their day? Learn the price of returning to first motions. Learn about those people, for the path they trod has long been forgotten.

It is not wise to tread this path unless you can do nothing else. This is a plunge only for those who have run out of options.

Now let us clearly distinguish the difference between the run-of-the-mill house churches and those which are committed to changing the world.

PART II

Contrasting
Typical House Churches
With
Radical House Churches

4

Fifty-Seven Varieties
of House Churches

We live in a day when there exists a phenomenon: an attempt to return to the "primitive church." Yet, what is being born out of this phenomenon will not change present-day Christianity and is not a return to the primitive church. Countless Christians around the globe are seeing afresh that the modern practice of "church" is biblically groundless and spiritually ineffective. As a result, many have left the institutional church, and each group has returned to *one* of the first-century practices of meeting in homes. Let's look closely at the typical expression of this phenomenon, and then let's look at the radicals.

This phenomenon has been dubbed "the house church movement," but this is a misnomer.

The word "movement" conveys a unified motion among a specific group of people. This home church phenomenon is not a movement. Those who meet in homes consist of every stripe of Christian and represent every doctrinal pedigree. Consequently, there exists no monolithic movement. No set of house churches reflects all house churches. For these reasons, the phrase "house church movement" is misleading. House churches gather for many different reasons and focus on many different themes. These differences are so great that they end up placing many house churches galaxies apart.

The term "house church movement" places the emphasis on the wrong thing—the house. Granted, the location of the church meeting has significance, but what God is after goes far beyond *where* His people meet. To put it bluntly, there is nothing inherently magical about meeting in a house. While gathering in homes is better than gathering in basilicas, meeting in a home is not the hallmark of the ekklesia.

Let's look at . . .

House Church Subcultures

I have lived outside the reach of organized Christianity for the past thirteen years. Based on my experience, most of the groups that fly under the flag of "house church" or "New Testament church" can be categorized as follows:

The Glorified Bible Study

This brand of house church is typically chaired by an ex-clergyman or an aspiring Bible teacher. This person usually facilitates a round-table discussion of the Scriptures. Meetings are dominated by Bible expositions which often descend into fruitless debates. In the glorified Bible study, those members who are not theologically inclined have a rather thin participation. Whether he recognizes it or not, the person facilitating the Bible study is in charge of the church.

The Special Interest Group

These home groups make their focal point for assembling a common interest like home school, home birth, the keeping of Jewish feasts, a particular eschatological view, a pro forma pattern of church service, organic farming, personal prophecy, Holy Ghost laughter, social justice, or some other issue, fad, or thing—even house church itself!

The Personality Cult

Members of these groups center their universe around a gifted man or woman. It may be a dead apostle whose writings act as the exclusive medium for the group's identity, beliefs, and practices. More often, the object of attention is a Christian leader who founded the church and perpetually stays resident within it. While the gifted personality often has a genuine desire to see the body build *itself* up, his mere presence obstructs this spiritual dynamic. He is typically blind to the fact that he has unwittingly fostered a pathological dependence upon himself. He is, therefore, the son of the modern pastor.

The Bless-Me Club

At bottom, this is a narcissistic community—a spiritual ghetto. The meetings are insular and highly charismatic. The group functions as a spiritual fueling station for burned-out Christians in need of an emotional fix. Concentration on individual needs is the central focus. Its members typically bail out whenever the group faces a rough thicket. So when conflict or dry spells occur, those who were most zealous about "house church" end up being lured back to the polish and flair of the program-driven religious system.

The Socially Amorphous Party

These home groups are typically comprised of four to eight people who nebulously meet in a living room to chat over tea and cookies. They rarely attain critical mass because they lack vision and purpose. They like to speak bulbously about Jesus being present whenever "two or three are gathered together." However, they usually fold before they even begin to understand why they exist. If they do not fold, their meetings become progressively sterile as the years roll by.

The Disgruntled Malcontent Society

Comprised of ex-church derelicts and recycled Christians, these groups happily assemble to lick their wounds and slam the "spiritually abusive" institutional church. Their meetings are permeated with an atmosphere of pessimism, cynicism, and veiled bitterness. Tragically, after the members tire of attacking the organized church, they begin to chew one another up. Thus they find themselves taken by the same spirit they set out to oppose. This form of house church attracts Christians who are deeply wounded and have not learned to trust others.

The Unwritten-Liturgy-Driven Church

These groups clearly stand outside the stream of institutional Christianity, but they often do not meet in a home. Many gather in a rented building or a "meeting hall." The dominating weakness of their gatherings is the lurking presence of an unwritten liturgy. The ironclad liturgy, which is practiced perfunctorily every week, is never questioned or changed. In fact, if the order of worship is broken in any way, the leadership of the church will call the violators on the carpet to reprove them for their irreverence!

All of these groups happily sail under the banner of "house church" or "New Testament church," yet they all fall short of the scriptural ekklesia. By New Testament standards, an ekklesia is a group of Christians who gather unto, by, and for the Lord Jesus Christ alone. It is an assembly of believers who are fiercely committed to Christ's full expression in their community. Jesus Christ is the life-blood of the ekklesia. He is the center. He is the circumference. He is the content. He is the focus. He is the sole gathering point of the church.

The saints who gather as an ekklesia are consumed with Jesus Christ and nothing else. Their goal is to make Him visible in their community. Their hallmark is their growing knowledge of the Lord, and their testimony is an unmistakable love for one another. House churches that are not characterized by these spiritual features not only miss a step, but they dance the wrong dance.

A genuine ekklesia is neither issue-centered, person-centered, or doctrine-centered. It is Christ-centered! The ekklesia exists for one purpose and one purpose alone: the unveiling of the centrality and supremacy of her Lord! In fact, in God's view the ekklesia is a person, not a structure. It is Jesus Christ in corporate human expression (Acts 2:47; 5:14; 9:4; 1 Cor. 12:12).

The Peril Of A Short Shelf Life

It is quite telling to note that many modern house churches disintegrate over a brief time span. According to my observations over the past thirteen years, the typical house church has an average life span of six months to four years.

Within this six-to-four-month window, the church usually dissolves due to an irreconcilable split or an unresolved crisis. (The crisis is usually rooted in a high-drama power struggle, a sustained bickering over hobby-horse theology, or an unwillingness to forbear with intractable personalities.)

If the group manages to hold together through the thrall of such conflict, it usually drifts toward a scaled-down "small-is-beautiful" version of the institutional church. That is, someone from within the group will devolve into the near-equivalent of a modern pastor. This person may not be called the pastor, and he may not act like an authority-monger. But he will function like a professional cleric, and the saints will grow to over-depend upon him.

The other likely result is that a group of men who tag themselves elders will surface and rule the church in oligarchical fashion—running roughshod over everyone else's sensibilities. In these respects, scores of modern house churches have failed to rid themselves of the old leaven of authoritarianism.

Granted, there are house churches that push past the four-year mark, but they are rare. It is still rarer to find a house church that has been in existence for over ten years. House churches that have been extant over twenty years are an endangered species. And house churches that have over twenty years of mileage are lamentably scarce.

In short, when Jesus Christ is not the center of a house church, the only fuel that can drive it is a charismatic personality, a fascinating issue, or a nifty doctrine. All of these fuels yield low mileage; and when they run dry, the group collapses.

A fellowship of believers can only be held together in any operative way when a continual encounter with the Lord Jesus becomes the dominating element. At bottom, if Christ is not the glue of a non-institutional church, its meetings will become shallow, colorless, and eventually unsustainable.

Uncovering A Mammoth Flaw

Let me press the thorny question: Why have so many house churches bitten the dust? I believe a large piece of the reason is that they were not founded upon a revelation of the Lord Jesus Christ. They were founded upon something less.

There are a raft of things today that Christians assemble around—even noble things that have something to do with Christ. But there is a colossal difference between meeting around some *thing about* the Lord and meeting around the Lord Himself! There is a vast ocean between meeting around an "it" and meeting around "Him"!

The Psalmist once uttered,

If the foundations be destroyed, what can the righteous do?

Ps. 11:3

If you were to read your New Testament with an eye for discovering how the early ekklesias were formed, you would find that they were solidly built upon the unshakable revelation of Jesus Christ (Matt. 16:16-18). All the ekklesias that Paul planted were built upon this revelation (1 Cor. 3:3). They were all rooted upon a ground-breaking unveiling of what he called "the mystery" (Col. 4:3; Eph. 1:17-22; 6:19).

What is this mystery? In short, the mystery is the unfolding of God's eternal purpose concerning His Son. Paul uncorked this glorious mystery to whoever would listen; and out of this mighty unveiling of the mystery of God, ekklesias were spontaneously born. (Note that the declaring of Jesus Christ has in it community-forming properties.)

The ekklesia founded upon the Lord Jesus Christ can survive under the most intense pressure and testing (1 Cor. 3:6-15). The winds may blow brutally and the floods fall fiercely, but the house will stand because it is founded upon a Rock (Matt. 7:24-27; Luke 6:46-48). Put another way, Jesus Christ is the only unmovable foundation upon which God's people may rightfully gather.

Tragically, few Christians in our day have any idea of what the mystery of God is nor of how all-encompassing it was to Paul. Notwithstanding, the mystery of God's eternal purpose is the central thought of the entire Scripture. Paul's letters are literally dripping over with the phrase. (1 Cor. 2:6-3:2; Rom. 16:25-26; Col. 1:24-27; 2:1-3; 4:2-3; Eph. 1:9-10; 2:14-16; 3:1-11; 5:29-32; 6:19).

If your group is seeking to serve God without the sturdy props of human hierarchy, you must build your community life upon the mystery of God in Christ. If you do not, your chances of surviving are close to nil. What you have just read is all too typical of most house churches. Do you see these churches as anything near what we need on the earth today?

Now, what does the radical house church look like in contrast?

5

The Radical Wing of the House Church Movement

Let's look at the other side of the house church movement—the radical house churches. (And they are much more than just house churches.) In other words, let's look at the side of the house church movement which is radical—not only radical, but daring. And intent on change—change that pales the Reformation. Change that covers every aspect of what is called church.

Some things are hard to describe, but let me try.

The layman is first; he is also second; and he is also last, and everything in the middle. The clergy? Normally, one would say "the clergy is last"; but, in fact, among us he is non-existent.

We are so used to having a clergy that the very thought of its not existing in the church is virtually incomprehensible to the Christian mind. Churches are needed which are a radical break from the norm.

Such churches need to be raised up by workers, but by a new breed of workers. There are workers in the radical house churches, yes. But . . .

But those workers are itinerant. They themselves are laymen. Their presence in one of the house churches is infrequent after the church is well-established. Their influence on the churches they work with is, unless there is a crisis, minimal . . . and always temporary!

Repeat: The worker is himself a layman. That includes: He works for a living.

Most of all, the man or woman who is a worker has been approved by the brothers and sisters in the church in the city where he works for a living. That fact needs a little explanation, as it is a new wrinkle.

Perhaps the best way to illustrate this is to recount the story of the Iroquois Indians. The Iroquois Indians had a unique way of choosing the chiefs and the other leaders of their tribe. The women chose those who would be the leaders of the tribe!

That is not exactly our own experience, but it is close. (It is not just the women who decide, it is everyone.) The church herself approves who will be workers. (It is not particularly considered a great honor!) When you are a Christian living in community—especially in community where there is endless freedom—there comes into being some very hardheaded realism. No one is striving to be an elder. (The thought of being stuck with being an elder is horrifying.) For most of us, the thought of being a worker only elicits pity.

Nevertheless, consider this: The men who help the churches are men who first lived in church life . . . before becoming workers. They were ordinary, everyday, brothers, well-known by the churches they were in. No secrets about their capacities or inabilities, their strengths and weaknesses. These men are known—through and through. These men are not considered special by anyone. These are the people who will go out and help the churches. In church life, these men passed through a great deal of exposure before being recognized as workers. They know how to have church life. They are ready to face problems. Their solutions are based on bedrock realities.

Do you realize, this way of having workers removes the mystique of the clergy? Do you realize what it is like to be a worker who is known through and through, by everyone? He is not treated special. No one thinks of him as a spiritual giant or as someone who has secret spirituality no one else has. He is simply a brother who helps churches.

Remove the mystique of the minister, and you are on your way to a new breed of workers.

I repeat: Every man who serves one of these radical churches is a layman. He is known through and through. And before he ministers, he has spent years in church life.

Let's look further at this incredible new world of ministry.

The mystique of the clergy has its origin in the fact that the minister went to the seminary. Somewhere along the way, while in seminary, he is supposed to have become a spiritual giant.

He walks into a church as their new pastor. On that day, no one present knows anything about him—neither his strengths nor his weaknesses. God's people have no idea of his spiritual insight (or lack thereof). This not only can, but almost always does, lead to disaster. Not only disaster for the poor laymen and women, but also disaster for the poor minister. In the institutional church there is a mutual destruction going on.

I don't think there is a layman on earth who has any idea how poorly prepared for any kind of ministry a seminary graduate is on the day he graduates from the seminary. Disaster awaits the minister—in any church—on the day he becomes the new pastor. In any institutional church there is a core group of locals who more or less run the church. They can be very cruel to the minister. (He is not a permanent fixture you know.) On the other hand, a minister standing in the pulpit can be extremely cruel to his parishioners as he teaches them legalism, do's and don'ts, and, alas, threatens them with the Bible's demands and God's wrath.

Such things do not happen in our world of radical churches. Out here in the sunlit plains of reality, workers could not get away with such, not for five minutes. Everyone knows everyone. Everyone is aware of everyone's strengths and weaknesses. Not only do God's people in church life know the worker through and through; he, in turn, knows the brothers and sisters he will be working with . . . through and through.

Both worker and people know the cross. We know the cross because we have experienced it. (All of us have experienced it because we've lived in community!) When we preach the cross, it is because the preaching of the cross has come out of our own experience.

When we share the depths of Jesus Christ, it is because we have touched the depths of Jesus Christ—both worker and everyone else. When we give practical suggestions to the church, it is because we have received practical help ourselves, . . . perhaps long ago . . . as ordinary brothers in the church do. The insights given, the help we bring, have nothing to do with theory. We have previously experienced that of which we speak.

Instead of there being a mutual destruction, there is mutual edification. The brothers and sisters strengthen the worker and encourage him because they know and love him as though he were their next-door neighbor. (Back before he became a worker, somewhere in an ekklesia, he was someone's next-door neighbor.)

This brother who itinerantly ministers, in turn, gives practical help to the body. He gives help in the regular meetings, in the smaller meetings, and in things which go on outside the meetings. There stands a brother everyone knows, and he has been through the crucible of church life.

I believe these men to be the best prepared, best trained, most spiritually competent ministers on this planet—and the most worthy of your trust.

Let's take a closer look at the radical house churches which these workers raise up.

6

Taking the Harder, Higher Route

When we see a house church being born, we see it born in freedom. The rules, the rituals, the regulations are all stripped away. Can you understand that freedom makes church life three times more difficult than it is in most of the churches in the house church movemen?

God's people are free. This is dangerous. And wonderful. God's people are free to do whatever they wish. They are free to join together to know and worship Jesus Christ.

They are free to cause a bellyful of problems. Or, to put it another way, free to be found out. There is no sense of legalism. No one is telling anyone else what he should or should not do.

Obviously we have not chosen an easy way: (1) community, (2) freedom, (3) no professional leaders, (4) no peripheral doctrines, (5) no organizational structure, (6) no legalism, (7) Christ paramount in message, sharing and experience.

A roomful of free-swinging laymen and laywomen all expressing their opinions about everything. Ah! Now this is life.

When a man or a woman falls madly in love with Jesus Christ, legalism becomes as obsolete as a buggy whip on a supersonic jet.

All this may be difficult to grasp; it may even be difficult to believe. On the other hand, what would you expect from a revolution? If you do have doubts, please come visit us. Find out for yourself. You will find no sense of legalism or conformity. (If while visiting you happen to run into any such things, it is most likely coming from someone who just recently arrived!) There is little chance that anyone who is a worker will be lording it over the church . . . there is too much freedom present for someone to try to overlay any kind of legalism or rules . . . or guilt.

It gets worse . . . or better . . . depending on how you've handled this book so far. So hold on, there is more.

The general concept of what a church is (especially in the house church) is that everyone comes into the living room, sings a few songs, studies the Bible, guided by a leader or leaders, shares a few things, and then everyone goes home.

Our concept of the church is that when you come into a meeting, it is for Christ. You cannot find the leader in the meeting. No one is looking to anyone to lead. The reason you cannot find the leader is because he does not exist. Then where does leadership come from? It comes from the brothers' meetings, it comes from the sisters' meetings, and it comes from the meetings. It also comes out of the groundswell of living together. That might sound impossible, but that is why we speak of . . . revolution! What is happening is revolutionary. We would to God that every Christian could know such freedom and know the joy of seeing a church in which everyone functions in the gatherings.

As I said, it gets worse.

We have fun! Lots of it.

What do I mean by that?

I mean things like: a weekend when all the women are together, and they have fun—maybe even pillow fights or water balloon fights; and a weekend when all the men are together and spend the whole time teasing one another. And both these weekends will probably be interspersed with time spent with Christ. Or odd things might happen, like calling off all meetings for two weeks and having fun instead of regular meetings. Canceling a couple of weeks of the meetings, so that we can have more time to spend with one another! And with the Lord. And we have banquets! Lord's Supper meetings are sometimes banquets—and they are always simply too wonderful to describe. Laughter in all the meetings. Speakers getting interrupted by questions, insights, responses . . . and wit.

Brothers' meetings in which the brothers spend half the meeting convulsing with laughter. Sisters' meetings in which there is the Lord's presence, and others in which they plan things to surprise the brothers. (Or they may be plotting against them!)

The women planning out a drama, presentation or skit and then presenting it in a meeting. Sometimes the skit is the meeting. The rest of us watch and either laugh or cry all the way through, or both.

Sometimes everyone in the church gets dressed up and takes in the theater and dinner at a restaurant.

You are familiar with a "toast" for someone you respect. We have "roasts" instead. We do this often, and we laugh 'til we cry.

And yes, we are saved, and, yes, we are Christians. These are hallmarks of a people who are free in Christ, yet a people who love Him with a passion, and know Him intimately.

And never forget: Meetings are centered totally on the Lord Jesus Christ.

Again, these things are not easy to imagine. From afar you might wonder about such a church; but one thing we have always asked of believers who are interested: Come and see. Come and spend a weekend with us. Be in our meetings. Watch. Listen. Ask.

Now, to the problems—problems in the typical house churches and how they are handled, contrasted with the radical churches.

PART III

The Dream Church
The Dream Work
The Dream Community

7

The Church, the Dream
and the Dreamer

Many kinds of people walk through that living room door. Each one of them has some kind of an agenda. And those who say they have no agenda have one as big as anyone else.

Why is this? Because every one of us has preconceived ideas as to what a *real* church ought to be. One person is looking for a social experience. Another evangelism. Another signs and wonders. Another, simply a place of comfort and sweetness. Another is looking for a sense of self worth. Some want to live in community, but do not want the church. (Yes, that is possible.) Perhaps—amazingly—a few have stepped through that door solely for the purpose of getting to know the Lord!! On the other hand, some, shocking as it may seem, come *only* to disrupt, criticize and condemn.

Every person who walks through that door has some sort of desire for something, and eventually that person will get around to insisting on *that* view. Here is a fact which threatens to destroy the brotherhood, the bond of peace, and the entire spectrum of the Christian life.

Perhaps all who come through the door *are* looking for the church, but for most it is a fantasy church they are looking for. Every person has a fanciful view of what community should look like, what the brotherhood should be, what ekklesia life is, and what a house church ought to be.

There is always the possibility of a head-on collision between this fantasy and the survival of the gathering.

In the beginning, there simply is no way to have total clarification of all that *is* and all that lies ahead. In the early stages of church life, the church *will* be groping its way along. (Not only in the beginning, but quite possibly until the very day you die.) The ekklesia is not an idea, a philosophy, or concept. The nature of the ekklesia is elastic, adaptable, changing and indefinable. Organic. Forever unfinished. Yes, and always defying definition.

Putting all the ducks in a row is her nemesis. She is divine reality. And she is not tame. Nor is she an organization, nor given to being organized.

She is neither a physical nor a psychological entity. This girl is a spiritual reality. She lives. She breathes. She has growth. She has a biological drive and genetic destiny. And you cannot define her nor can you predict her ways.

Dietrich Bonhoeffer observed:

> Innumerable times a whole Christian community has broken down because it has sprung from a "wish dream."

When you sit down in a meeting for the first time, you may have come with a very well-defined, clearly-thought-out concept of Christian community and a clear picture in your mind concerning ekklesia. There is a possibility that you will fight very hard to make sure this group becomes exactly what you envision. Fortunately, there are other people in that room who have *other* strong opinions as to what the body of Christ should be. And these views all conflict.

The fantasy church will not work and is doomed *everywhere except in your imagination*. If God does not bring such a church to an end, the people will! And then? Try again, on another street, in another house church, and you will meet the same results. You and everyone else will be overwhelmed. You and the others will be discouraged, defeated and disillusioned.

The fantasy church will never exist in the real world. It is so very, very easy to dream of what the church should be, but it will never get off the stage of your imagination. Nor can you afford to pay enough professional actors to play out all the roles the way you envision people should act while in church life. Be sure of one thing: God's people will *never* play out those roles for you. Your rapturous dream is impossible because of the fall, impossible because of human reality. Your castle in the sky is beyond the stretch of all mortals. Be informed: God's people have a nasty reputation of not playing out *anyone's* dream of church life. Historically, God's people are *very* uncooperative. You doubt? Ask Moses in the Old Testament. Ask Paul in the New Testament.

One of the growing pains of a body of people gathering together is the shedding of the fantasy church. But thank God it is out of this crisis that there grows hardheaded bedrock reality.

What emerges out of such raw reality? Neither *you nor anyone else* will ever have your perfect, fanciful church. God Himself will build *His* own foundation and His house. The sooner the disillusionment of the dream church crashes and dies, the better off the church.

> A community which cannot bear this
> crisis will forever lose the promise
> of Christian community.

Keep the fantasy and lose the community. Church life is an adventure into learning the spiritual nature, the organic nature, of the bride of Christ.

(And you believe *you don't* need outside help?)

You and every person who walks through that door must ask a simple question: Which do I hold more dear—my fantasy church, my dream, or the church herself?

You have no idea how furiously a man can hold to his views!

Which is more important, the dream or Christian brotherhood?

One of the first things God's people should learn is to lose. The church is built on loss.

Now, hold your breath for this next one.

It is a truism that the person who wants church life the most is frequently the one who later causes the most problems. The person who wants church life the most is sometimes the one who, in his zeal, destroys. Thank God this is not always true; but true it is frequently.

The fantasy church has no cords that can hold it together. If you see your dream not coming to reality, does that mean you leave community . . . or worse . . . seek to destroy what is there? In the past many have destroyed what was there. In the future this will continue to happen.

Learn this now. In the beginning you will be surrounded by pettiness. You will dwell in the midst of Christians who have incredibly thin skin. This you did not expect, but this *is* real. This does *not,* however, mark the end of the gathering. It marks *God's* starting place.

In those hours when you are seeing your dream fade, open your heart to Christ and learn of His riches, His mercies, and His patience. Eventually there emerges a very beautiful girl, even the expression of Christ's own wife.

8

Community, a Disaster Unless . . .

Most of those in the house church movement do not realize that a house church automatically throws God's people into *community*. And neither the institutional church nor the run-of-the-mill house church is ready for community. Community is a prescription for disaster for virtually every church, yet community automatically comes with house churches.

Community is not known in the institutional mindset, nor in the minds of most house church leaders. These leaders have no idea what awaits them when *community emerges*. Problems in community are far more prevalent than they are in the go-to-church-on-Sunday-and-never-get-to-know-anyone practice.

Men who start house churches but who are not prepared to handle the onslaught of problems which ensue can be recognized by how many laws and rules they introduce *and* how frequently they use the term *church discipline*.

House church leaders who have not lived in community—and lived in it for years—have no knowledge of the Pandora's box they open when community manifests itself. Further, they have absolutely no way to address the problems growing out of community living. Why be surprised at their inability to cope with this avalanche of interpersonal conflict. They never *lived* in community. Most house church leaders do not even know what community is. They have no knowledge of community and little or no knowledge of the cross. And you think *you* can raise up a living, breathing church of the living God?

Be advised: When we enter the house church, we begin dealing with fallen creatures at *close range*. If there is not a long-term work of transformation in all these people, then somewhere along the way the flesh emerges . . . in spades. Because there is a void of the working of the cross in their lives, because there is no worker qualified to address the problems that arise—that is, problems in the church which he has never seen before—God's people end up being deeply hurt. The house church movement, as a whole, will *die* from lack of knowing the "how" of church life.

Are you prepared to enter a world of untested workers, a crossless people, community with no one who has previously known community, a church in which community has no spiritual depth and no knowledge of how to tread that path? I beg you to know, there are higher, better ways to Christ and to the church.

Now a word to workers and to would-be workers outside the institutional church. Flesh and lack of experience living in *community* will destroy the new, the wonderful, the spontaneous work.

9

Community in Reality

To put it quite simply, Christians need Jesus Christ and Christians need other Christians. In both cases: *at close proximity.*

In Jesus Christ we are one, yes, and we are also intended to be gathered under a roof . . . sharing that oneness. And in Him we are touching a fellowship like that which is in the other realm.

You will not be long in this gathering before you make a very interesting discovery: You are an alien on this planet. (This planet is not following Christ.) Long ago a fallen species left a garden and spread across the earth. This fallen species is in control of the activity on this planet . . . everywhere *except* in this "colony of heaven" . . . that is, except in the body of Christ; that is, the community of believers, the ekklesia. She is the only exception. She is the only exception.

You are part of a different species. This species had its origin *not on this* planet, but in other realms. And the habitat of this species is the *church,* not the world. The church of Jesus Christ is a chip of heaven come to earth. At this moment you cannot transport your soul and your body to the other realm. But your spirit can go there. When you meet together with other "aliens" you are immediately drawn to them. There is an instinct in you and in them to gather with one another. You even sense you have known these people in some other realm, in a place called the eternals.

A parallel illustration of this natural drawing to one another can be seen in what Americans do when they move to a foreign nation. They immediately search out a colony of their kind. When people leave their nation they automatically find a colony of their nationality. Kind of their kind. So too Christians, by nature, looks for other believers! You and I are driven to be with other believers. Once we touch "this colony of heaven," we find we are aliens even in the land of our birth.

You need other believers. If for no other reason, you need other believers because *you are a believer!* Through the act of regeneration, you have been biologically altered. Because of the redemption process of Jesus Christ, you have instincts and drives unique to the Christian species. Part of you belongs in another realm. That unique part of you will forever *drive* you toward community . . . that is, toward *church life.*

Unfortunately, community is virtually unknown today. The only thing a Christian knows to be the "church" is a pew, a steeple, a service, and a sermon. There is no visible fellowship in such an arrangement. There is no divine encounter to be seen and known by believers with seeking hearts.

What else is blatantly missing?

Functioning!

By her very nature, the ekklesia is a gathering where *everyone* present *functions*. That is unprecedented. Worldwide, that is unprecedented.

If there is no free flow of functioning in the meeting, there is no church at all. The kingdom of God calls for a church that is beautiful and glorious, but the kingdom of God also calls for a church aggressive and moving forward. The church is a free-flowing, functioning people.

This is a thought so foreign to most that it is impossible to explain what it is like in practice. We hear visitors to our meetings say: "I've never seen anything like this." A divine fingerprint is on a gathering where all function and the topic is Christ. Without that fingerprint the group will die. Functioning that is *Christ* causes *life* to flow. Functioning that is death obviously kills.

Among the thoughts no one has when they think of church is "every member functioning." The idea of a body functioning—in all the meetings—nonexistent. And a call you have probably never heard, nor will you ever likely hear from any pulpit is a call to community. Not from a pulpit! Community and the Protestant practice of "church" are two worlds which never meet.

There are two flawed assumptions abounding in this day: (1) that you need no constant touch with Jesus Christ outside the meetings, and (2) that "this house church stuff is going to be easy."

Ask an experienced group what happens to Christians when they "just get together every week" without a fresh flow in their lives. Then ask these same people if church life is easy.

To look to anyone who is a theorist is to embrace disaster. Further, beware the man bearing *verses*. A person who has known genuine church life will *not* be bearing verses or theory. He will be bringing you Christ.

Have you presumed that having the house church is easy? Then consider this: The eccentricities of the psychopath always come as fixtures with *every* house church. Let us not forget the man who would be dictator. (From time to time there comes a man to the group who would even be *god*.) Then there is the self-appointed person who is going to *stop* the would-be god by any means, fair or foul.

10

Solutions

What can be done to overcome the flaws we encounter in the house church movement?

What does the house church movement need? For starters, an understanding that the prevalent movement lacks an interest in a deep walk with Jesus Christ.

Knowing Christ deeply does not seem to be part of the Christian mind. This must change. Only a move from being Bible-centered to being Christ-centered can save us from the dubious honor of being like the past. (We will in no way neglect Scripture. We will use it far more than most Christians do, but our focus will be Jesus Christ.)

Is the Lord Jesus Christ so superficial that we can be justified in neglecting Him in favor of other things? Have we so quickly exhausted the unsearchable riches of Christ that we must move on to lesser topics? Or perhaps we think there are loftier subjects than the Lord Jesus? If so, we have far surpassed Paul of Tarsus! The man who started his spiritual life with a blinding revelation of Jesus Christ is seen at the end of his life crying out to know Him. Paul had a great initial revelation, "caught up in the third heaven," but with all that, at the end of his life he knew nothing, compared with what there is to be known.

What does the house church movement need to be? Desperate. Needy. Hungry. Thirsty. Not for truths, not for New Testament patterns, not for Bible knowledge. For a Man! Hungry to know our Lord! Read church history, and you will see that this reality is neither known nor spoken of by the institutional church, and certainly it is not in the house church movement as it is generally practiced.

Jesus Christ must not be relegated to being another static topic within the Christian faith. Let that stop now! May the Lord, in His grace, give us experience of a matchless Son who is the center and reason and purpose of the Father. Then the house church will turn this old world on its ear.

What does the house church movement need to be? A people drawn together by nothing save the Lord Jesus Christ . . . paying attention to this undiscovered Man in the Glory. In Him is the residue of all the riches of both realms seen and unseen. This just might be worth giving up all the issues we currently gather around.

Repeating: The house church movement needs to place more time, more enthusiasm, more zeal and more energy into knowing Jesus Christ deeply than it does on Bible study, evangelism, home schooling, women's roles, or community living. Little foxes keep us distracted from Him! Let's quit those things that seem to be "it," quit them cold turkey. Lay aside "it" and pursue Him.

May it be so now, in this hour. Let's acknowledge that the typical Christian's relationship to the Lord is mostly theoretical, never having deep encounter with Him. Throughout the world, what Christians know of Christ is either what they have read or what they have heard. The Christian family has been deprived of the joys of discovering His interior presence. We have arrived at a point in time when many Christians are not content with just reading about John's and Paul's experiences with Christ. The stream of their writing moves beyond the words they wrote and flows to the reality of what they penned. Christ! Christ known! First-hand. Deeply. Daily. Internally.

As Manfred Haller, author of *Christ, All in All*, wrote:

> It can come as quite a shock to realize that you have believed in an idea of Christ and not in Christ Himself.

Let there be a people on the earth again who seek a profound, radical, eye-popping revelation of Jesus Christ. Then, in our meetings, you will see Christians never running out of things to say of His inexhaustible riches. Watch Christians come to know Him deeply, then you will hear them speak of Him in every meeting. Christians will stop speaking of things and start speaking of Him. Christians who encounter Him cease speaking about Him and begin speaking Him.

Generally, what is the topic of house church gatherings: (1) An "it," (2) the Bible, (3) something about Him, or (4) Him? Let's go beyond the things of God to God Himself. Knowing and expressing Christ Himself is the soil of true church life. Here is the difference between being the ekklesia of the Living God or merely meeting in a house.

A cure for the eighteen-hundred-year-old lack of spiritual depth did not magically appear with the house church movement.

> Drinking in a deep spiritual revelation of Jesus Christ is the only chance house churches have for survival.

What else? The worker. The itinerant Christian worker. The church planter. As a whole, the house church movement has rejected a return to this primitive and pivotal figure. The strange part is that he figures so plainly in Scripture—a fact the house church movement, no matter how Bible study centered it is, refuses to recognize.

There has been a brief mention of the disappearance of hundreds of house churches every year. Let's look a little closer and see just how unprepared the typical house churches are for the problems they encounter when Christians get in close proximity to one another.

11

The Disappearance of House Churches Every Year

House churches collapse and disappear faster than they are born. Thousands of little groups varying in size from four to fifty are born and disappear with every passing day. The increase in the number of churches is *zero*. Yet, every year these beautiful little groups say, "God will take care of us. He will not let this happen to *us*." But it does. Virtually every house group will last no more than six months to three years.

Why?

Two major reasons.

Number One: The leader is local.

Number Two: The leaders are inexperienced . . . even if they appear to be *very* experienced. It is a difference of the mindset. Are they experienced in the institutional mindset or in that of radicals? They never lived in a successful *surviving* house church before leading a house church. The few such groups that do survive do so because a person arises who takes over leadership (perhaps becomes a dictator).

(These are pastors. A rose by any other name is still a pastor.) Later comes a church building. Then follows "order of service," etc. Alas, the group ends up being an institutional church.

Are there any exceptions? Generally speaking, *no*. This is a *house group holocaust*. And what can prevent this massive destruction?

Someone who comes to help from outside—but does not stay—is the best answer. That is an *itinerant* worker.

But even here, there is a great risk. There are so many unqualified people willing to come to you. Often these men end up remaining with the group, becoming the leadership. The concept of the traveling—itinerant—worker, a man coming to them to help temporarily, is quite literally a thought foreign to all. A truly radical idea!

Apart from the *itinerant worker*, what else brings down a house group?

The words of Dietrich Bonhoeffer give us an opening clue.

> It is not to be taken for granted that a Christian has the privilege of living among other Christians.

To press the point, it is virtually impossible for Christians to live among Christians!

Long ago, Jesus Christ lived among a group of Christians. The end result? All his followers disappeared at the sight of the cross. The sight of the cross will always cause people to pause and rethink . . . *everything*!

Let it be said that when a Christian is living among Christians, he may soon come to see them as "enemies if they were in any other circumstances." The *fall of man* has kept church life that lasts from being easy!

Community and the cross tend to intermingle.

Now, let's talk about farms. Yes, farms! Most every year we hear of an entire group of Christians who decide to move out to a farm, get away from the world, grow organic carrots, raise their children by home schooling and, at the same time, call themselves *the church*. (To those Christians who are foolish enough to build a house on that farm without owning the ground it sits on, you are courting disaster.)

The group will sunder. The Christian world has not the remotest idea of how a group of people can live next door to one another in peace. Actually it is not possible for Christians to live that near one another without disaster.

Unless!

Unless ingredients not known by most of the Lord's people and the Lord's workers are added to the mix.

Why this trail of unrelenting disaster? When problems arise, the group or its leaders look for tangible, visible, physical, local solutions. Alas, this is the wrong place to look. All solutions have to do with realms unseen. Just how far do people go in underestimating the difficulty of community? To the 20th power![1] The present practice of the Christian faith is not endued nor equipped with the elements needed for Christians to live with one another at close quarters.

There simply is no evangelical history of this. Evangelical understanding of community is zero. Further, those poor souls who cloister themselves out on a farm are totally outside the Christian manifesto and the church's Magna Carta. We do belong together, but the ekklesia belongs in the thick of the reality of this world. We may not be of the world, but we are still *in* the world. Moving to an isolated place is not church life, and it is *not* a solution. It is also without scriptural precedent. It is a recipe for devastation.

In Jesus Christ we have been made one, but finding how to make the reality of that oneness

---

[1] Imagine enough zeros to fill an encyclopedia.

practical is met with about the same results as a man running a marathon with one foot in a glue pot.

From the day Jesus ascended until the day when He shall return, it has been given to us to be a real, practical, *visible* ekklesia in the world. This word *ekklesia* does not refer to some ethereal concept out there in the stratosphere. Ekklesia is a visible fellowship, a community. If you please . . . a *civilization!*

That fellowship, that ekklesia, can be located, seen, attended. You can know the names of the people who gather. Further, that ekklesia has destiny and is carrying out the entire charter of the church. She is not a club, a people coming together to comfort and bless one another. She still kicks down the gates of hell.

Ekklesia is a people who almost literally live in one another's coat pocket on a daily basis. Furthermore, there is hardly a sentence in the New Testament, after the day of Pentecost, but what that sentence was addressed to a corporate body . . . *not* to an individual. If any sentence was written to an individual, that individual was still in the community of the ekklesia. It never crossed the mind of a first-century believer that he would live his life independent and outside of that visible fellowship, that community. (Anywhere you live except within that visible fellowship, you are living in a foreign country.)

When one isolated Christian, banished to Patmos, heard from the Lord, what the Lord said to that man was, "Write a letter to the *churches*." Always the ekklesia.

In the greatest chapter in the letter to Romans (Chapter 8), all the references to "you" are to an "all of you." The entire book of Romans is addressed to the corporate you. The only singular pronouns are two references to "I," and they refer to the author of the letter. There are over sixty plural pronouns. Every blessing, every exhortation, every admonishment, every encouragement, every spiritual truth, were written to a corporate body—a visible gathering of believers who were fellowshipping with Christ.

Further, every word you find in Chapters Twelve through Fifteen is to the body of Christ—a litany of statements dealing with the problems which arise out of life together. Chapter Sixteen of Romans is composed of a greeting to people who are involved in that corporate adventure of the community in Rome.

It is a biological instinct of Christians to be physically present with other Christians. The only purpose for that biological drive, that living together, is to bring forth the church of Jesus Christ.

You must ask, is my end desire to meet in a house with Christians who do no more than take care of one another, who speak to one another gently and

PART IV

God's Orphan . . .
The Church

12

For What Purpose Does the Church Exist?

For over 1700 years she has been Christendom's ugly step child. No one dares to change "church." Most ideas of the church are insipid. Change church and resolve all the issues. Leave church as it is today and no issues will *ever* be resolved.

Get to know her as she really is. You will fall in love with her. We declare that she is central. She is *the* issue. The only issue. For the last 1700 years, for the next 1700 years, she is the one and only issue. Why is she here? What part does she play? Who is she? *What is her purpose?*

At first glance, it would seem to be a rather easy question to answer. Why does she exist? Many reasons are commonly given; here are a few:

- The church exists to reach a lost and dying world.

- The church exists to minister to the needs of hurting people.

- The church exists to have a moral influence on society.

- The church exists as the place for Christians to come and learn about God.

Sound familiar? These thoughts, and many more, are confidently asserted as the church's purpose on earth.

All are dead wrong!

The church may at times reach the lost world, minister to hurts, have a positive moral influence, etc., but that is not and never was the purpose of this lady named ekklesia.

Let us take a moment to examine these views.

Most Christians seem to think that the church is here on earth with a mission. We are constantly reminded from the pulpit and all other avenues of Christian practice that Jesus came to save the lost at any cost. It logically follows, then, that the church must serve the same purpose—to seek and rescue the lost. Could any purpose be more noble? Furthermore, if this worthy cause was good enough for Jesus Christ, how dare the church not extend herself, with all her strength, to this sinful, dying world?

That is not why the church is on earth.

The presupposition that Jesus' whole purpose is linked to man, the fall, redemption, and to other earthly matters—a *man*-centered purpose—is communicated to us the moment we become Christians. We are keenly unaware that past generations have passed on to us this man-centered view. Without ever questioning this view, most of our experience, and much of the church's action, is driven by this thought. We reason that if God sent His Son on this mission, then surely this must be our (Great) commission too.

Unless . . .

Unless He came to earth with an entirely different purpose in mind.

Is it possible that we, our leaders, and most of our forefathers have overlooked the main point of his coming to earth? Will today's Christian mindset even allow us to question the reason for the Lord's coming to earth or dare question the church's purpose on earth?

Consider this:

Jesus Christ came to earth with His Father's passion to gather man into something that no human being had ever even imagined, much less experienced. Permit yourself to take a fresh look, with a different and open mind. Consider, from a different perspective, the real reason Christ came to earth.

We all know, even if we have never thought about it, that the Father and the Son were together in union with one another from *before* the beginning of time. Jesus Christ did not have His beginning at the point of His birth in Bethlehem. "In the beginning . . ." refers to long, long ago. It implies some state or condition *before* the moment called "the beginning."

But does it matter that Christ existed *before*? What relevance does this fact have to the purpose of the church? It has *great* relevance.

What were the Father and the Son doing before they created? What was their relationship to one another? Asking these questions helps us to discover the answer to the question, "What is the purpose of the church?" The significance of the activity between the Father and Son cannot be overstated. As we pursue this all-important matter, we can be certain of a few undeniable facts:

- God's mind has never been fallen.

- God's purpose has never been tainted.

- God has never altered his plan.

Some teach that there is a *Plan B*. That is because we are coming up short on what His eternal plan really is.

If you and I as believers (and as the church) are ever to live in the divine matrix, it will be only as we discover a divine mindset which proceeds forth from an unfallen mind—a mind which is eternal, not earthly.

Whatever the Father and Son were doing *before* creation was pure and had purpose. (Therein lies the key to the divine mindset, the divine purpose.) There in the bosom of the Godhead was a desire . . . a desire for some *future* accomplishment. That divine desire has never been altered. From the outset, the Father and the Son had one mutual thought. That thought was *for one another*. They loved one another. All else proceeds from that point. From before the beginning, they loved one another and fellowshipped together. Herein is the nature, the organic nature, of God.

Allow that fact to permeate you.

Imagine: In this eternal setting there were no distractions, no other intentions. Just one another. Jesus Christ filled the thoughts of the Father, filling Him like a pleasing fragrance. The Father saturated the very heart and being of the Son.

What occupied their thoughts? What was their idea? What was their desire? *One another*. Not some experience, but one another. This was their very existence. Not doing, just partaking of one another.

And yes, they did *do* something. They fellowshipped. That was their *divine occupation,* enjoying one another.

Just as the sun radiates light onto the moon, and the moon re-radiates that light back to the sun, again and again, so in like manner the Father and the Son reflect and re-radiate one another. The sun and the moon represent, dimly, the relationship of the Father and the Son.

The fellowshipping of divinity was the divine intention. This was God's *plan.* This was His *pattern.*

With this as their divine matrix, what would the Father and Son plan for their future? If this fellowship characterized the very nature of the Father and the Son—from *before* the beginning—then God's plan *in creation* would be an extension of their experience. The difference would be only enlargement.

When God created Adam, the divine purpose took on visibility and began to unfold. The result? God the Father and God the Son increased their fellowship.

That fellowship now included man. (This expanded fellowship can be observed for a brief time in the Garden of Eden. Other glimpses also occur later.) Their fellowship, now opened to man, was not there to force a social, political, activist, or any other type of organization on earth. It was not to incite people to be consumed with programs to correct wrongs. God's purpose has always been about fellowship—fellowship in a divine setting. Earth's story—*man's* story—is about God expanding this unique, divine fellowship.

Some years ago, a missionary came to visit a church with which I was working. He believed God's primary concern was the salvation of sinners, and the church was therefore on a divine mission. He declared to me *his own* passion for saving the lost and the absolute necessity for the church to have the same obsession. Moreover, he felt that he and I (we ministers) *must ensure* that the church have a burden for evangelism—even driven by guilt if necessary. Why? Because he felt this to be God's purpose, *God's burden.*

In the face of his convincing barrage, I had but one response to him. I wish to share it with you.

What if a church was never given one sermon on "soul winning." Never given one message on missions. Never made to feel guilty about anything. Never told to "Go!" Rather, only Jesus Christ was preached—his relationship to His Father and His eternal desire to have everyone of us occupied with Him and nothing else. What if that group of people was encouraged to spend their lives occupied only with Jesus Christ and nothing else?

Imagine: a church never having a burden for anything except fellowship with Jesus Christ and Him alone! Would not that local gathering discover his heart, in deep and wondrous ways? And in that discovery she would naturally respond, as a bride to her groom, to the things that are on the Lord's heart. She would move forward with God's eternally purposed desire for expansion of fellowship. (Remember, the matrix of the Father and Son is only fellowship.)

Imagine a people occupied with the Man, Jesus Christ. Not the message. Not ministry. Not missions. But only with the Man, Jesus Christ. A people saturated with something that was an eternal origin. Is it possible that those same people would fellowship with the Lord and with one another simply because they became caught up in the divine experience? Not because they were stimulated, compelled or driven by *guilt*.

Now we return to the question. What is the church's purpose?

The church was never intended to be a work station. The church was never intended to be a sermon center. And the church was certainly never intended to be a producer of activists. Her purpose is much loftier than earthbound activities. The church's purpose? To be occupied. Her purpose is to be occupied with her Lord. She exists for the same reason as do God Almighty and His Son, Jesus Christ—to be occupied with *one another*! To be occupied with her Lord! And to be occupied with her Lord in one another!

Know this: There *are* such groups of Christians as I have just described. I have experienced a church with that singular occupation. After many years she is *still* so occupied. She has traveled the globe expanding this very fellowship, without ever being told to go forth!

How does an ekklesia get to that place without ever being admonished to "Go!"?

The answer is easy. Find a Christian worker preoccupied with Jesus Christ. With Christ and nothing else. *Nothing* else. Find a worker who will never distract the church from Jesus Christ. A worker who knows how to bring a people into an organic discovery of Jesus Christ. One who has previously experienced this occupation . . . who has lived with a group of people occupied with Christ.

That is absolutely vital! This worker must be someone who, even in a crisis, will give Christ and nothing else. Find someone who *will help* you abandon every mindset that is not as old as eternity past.

What next?

Begin to gather in such a way that leaves minimal opportunity for distractions. Make a decision, as the church, to pursue only Jesus Christ. Do not pursue having a soul-winning church, or spiritual warfare, or anything but Christ. Do not become preoccupied with praise or worship, or studying what the end of the world will be like.

Only Jesus Christ.

Then, armed with this *divine* purpose and with a divine mindset . . . together pursue your Lord. That people, that ekklesia, will learn Him, know Him. She, the ekklesia, will discover many things she would never otherwise know. Just as a child completely, organically discovers its physical and mental capabilities, so *she* also learns. So will you as a part of her. You will enter into your rightful place in the wondrous discovery of Christ and the church.

There is nothing like knowing and participating with the Father and the Son and with one another in:

- The divine occupation
- The divine preoccupation
- The eternal purpose
- God's one and only obsession.

13

Shall It Be a Return to the Ekklesia of the Living God or Just Another House Church?

Other than meeting in homes, there is virtually no resemblance between the early church and the modern house church movement.

I have met with Christians in homes throughout my adult life and lived in Christian community for the last ten years. I am part of the house church movement. The radical part!

The house church movement as a whole must be considered one of the most anemic phenomena on the Christian landscape. The good news is that it is not too late to see a turnaround. If we do not, the house church movement will be a distant memory.

Among many house churchers there is an almost mystical reverence for the house itself. One house church newsletter has on its logo a dove descending down the chimney of a house! This magical quality associated with the house seems to imply that simply holding meetings in a house some way guarantees spiritual quality. After the novelty has worn off, does it really matter, then, whether you meet in a building or a home? Not if what you practice in the church building and in the house are identical. Does meeting in houses make men radical? Is the house church movement like moviegoers who gave up viewing films in the theater and began watching them in homes? Is there a difference? This does not constitute a reformation, let alone a revolution! Church building Christianity equals death and boredom. Putting it in homes yields the same tragic result. Same foods, different pot.

Summing it up, house churches I have visited are having traditional church in someone's living room. A weak catalyst for revolution, and revolution is certainly what is needed.

The house church movement today has the same tired, old, dead mindset. The same dead practices of the last 500 years: local leaders, rituals, offices, tithes, clergymen, and a silent laity. It is also an elder-emphasizing movement. These have been tried and found wanting for generations. Why insist on these old ways? The typical house church is bent on emphasizing at least some of these: legalism, dogmatism, tongues, ecumenicalism, home schooling, elders, church discipline, covenanting, women's role in the church, social justices and liturgies!

With all of this theological chewing gum, when does Jesus Christ get our attention? Where does the bride of Christ, the church, have a chance to fulfill the purpose of her existence? Namely, in knowing and experiencing her Lord deeply, and in making Him known. And in her being visible to principalities and powers.

The larger part of the house church movement is driven by an engine of intellectualism. Consequently, the house church movement is doomed to fail. We need to change the frontal lobe view of a house church to a gathering that has a spiritual engine! Yes, it has a knowledge of Bible verses that is staggering. This is unquestionably the most Bible-centered . . . and Christ-neglected . . . age since the days of the Pharisees. The house church movement seems convinced that it will be able to overcome its lack of spiritual depth by working very hard to find out how the first-century churches operated. And then by duplicating it. Analysis, theory, formula are not ingredients for revolution.

The house church movement lacks an interest in knowing Christ or making Him central. Where is that recognition of another realm, of the unseen? What you see is an earthbound objectiveness in dire need of a sense of the eternals.

Most house churches have in their meetings a lack of transaction and interaction with the other realm. Having dinner together, sitting around sharing about our week and our beliefs is supposed to fill that spiritual vacuum? Most think that studying the Bible is a spiritual interest. (It is not!) Opinions, theorizing, parsing Greek words, dissecting, analyzing, postulating, and cogitating on sentence fragments do not constitute a spiritual church.

House churchers often state that the goal of their meetings is to have participation by everyone and to edify one another. That is a good starting place, but tea, cookies, a few personal testimonies, covering a Bible verse, and singing—that is not stuff of first-century meetings! Meetings in the early church were centered on Jesus Christ. Believers of that day knew that by gathering together they were satisfying some of their Lord's needs. His needs. The house church movement has little or no sense of what the needs of the Lord Jesus Christ are or of what God's eternal purpose is.

The typical testimony is "what the house church has done for me." If there is such a testimony, it is "I-centered" to the core. In general, the house church movement is "me-centered," it has a meet-my-needs mindset. It is a cerebral love affair with discovering "what is in it for me." The outcome: a self-centered people.

First-century gatherings were filled with a conscious depth. There was an encounter with the

Lord. This provoked the declarations of the risen, exalted, enthroned, glorified, living Jesus Christ.

Jesus Christ was, and always should be, the focus .. and the content .. of meetings. Jesus Christ has a physical presence through the members of His body. Such holy things do not typify most of the house church movement, yet this alone is the "how" of the Christian life. The content of first-century meetings resonated from the Spirit and found its hallmark in the spirits of those gathered. No study was going on.

Something as temporal as someone teaching facts about the Bible simply cannot ever result in the eternal matter of making Christ visible in the meetings of the church.

First-century folks were generally simple, uneducated folk. They would be mystified by the house church movement. Parsing Aramaic in their gatherings? A frontal lobe stimulation session? Mistaking debate for a spiritual encounter?

Like every Protestant movement before us, the house church movement is promoting an experience with the Bible instead of one with an indwelling Lord. Only a radical move to Christ will change Christianity.

Do we really believe that Bible study in a home is any more interesting or spiritual than it is in a building? With an illiteracy rate over 99% and books as rare as a three-horned cow, are we actually convinced that first-century believers sat around and studied the Bible? Even an elementary understanding of the setting and the context of the epistles of the New Testament renders the very notion of first-century Bible study as absurd. Yet, this is about as good as it gets in most house churches. The house church movement can be better. Incomparably better.

14

Meeting Needs –
Is This the Church?

Need-meeting gatherings are not the church of Jesus Christ, nor even a plausible substitute. Popular? Yes. Scriptural? No. First-century practice? Absolutely not!

Are these little groups wonderful to be a part of? Quite frankly, they are probably the most beautiful experience of *human* life ... at least for a few weeks. But once pressure is added, once responsibility is embraced, once the purpose of the church begins to be faced ... any of these ... then you discover that the foundation of that group *cannot* hold. That is because, in truth, there is no real foundation.

The leader is often a benign, gentle brother. *As long as no crises arise* this group can survive over a long period of time if someone has the rare gift of keeping the peace. To do this the leader will usually move heaven and earth to keep from allowing the group to get under pressure. The group's comfort zone must never be violated. If it is, everything shatters. Thousands of groups like this can accomplish nothing when they have so fragile a fabric.

The fellowship of the body of Christ, a visible, local, attendable gathering, should be so constituted that it can, and will, withstand storm, fury, the darts of Satan, and the eruptions of hell. But be assured such a group is exotically rare.

Also be assured that such a gathering experiences much blessing and much joy. Joy which springs up by no greater event than a brother's accidentally encountering another brother.

The riches found in such a life together are inexhaustible. Everyone in that ekklesia feels privileged for no reason except that they are living in the daily fellowship of divine life with one another. For this they see themselves as the most blessed of believers.

Has there been a time when you met with a group of Christians you felt had touched heaven? Be sure that if you should go farther and take the *long* journey in the ekklesia, there will be such joy.

Also be assured there will be moments of the cross. And yes, there will be moments when you are not sure that the community of believers you are gathering with *will* survive.

If you live in the manner your Lord intended believers to live, then you cannot be separated from community. The Christian life cannot be totally fulfilled, except that it be found within the realm of that visible fellowship. The Christian life does not really make sense, long term, except your life be lived out in the experience of the body of Christ.

PART V

The Institutional Church
vs.
The Most Beautiful
Girl in the World

15

Ever Changing,
Yet Always the Same

What keeps hope alive in the institutional church? A new fad *is* a new hope. Such fads come along about every three or four years. All are launched in a hope of changing institutional Christianity. Be advised: It is all a mirage. A fantasy. The present-day church still looks just like it did 500 years ago. The beginning of the Protestant era and the present Protestant era look just the same! Hundreds of fads, insights, doctrines, revivals, Bible schools, seminaries, home Bible classes . . . all renew hope that things will change. Hope upon hope, yet the institutional church looks just like it did half a millenium ago!

It is *not change* that must come. It is starting over—*radically* starting over! This is the vista before us.

Nothing that comes along in the institutional church will *ever* change the institutional church. In fact, the Catholic church is exactly like it was one thousand years ago, and the Protestant churches of a thousand years from now will look just like they do now. Those creaky old ways are here forever . . . fads, new ideas, new doctrines, new practices notwithstanding.

Change in what church is and how church is expressed will take place *only* outside the traditional church. If there is something which holds out the promise of change inside the organized church, *it will not* live up to its billing. The institutional practice of Christianity kills! It kills everything . . . that is, the institutional church kills *life*! Repeat: Anything claiming to change the institutional church *will* fail!!

Everything that will change Christianity will be done *outside* the traditional system. And it will be led by a new breed of workers and people with desperate hearts.

With that in mind, let us continue to search out this pivotal element: a new kind of Christian worker. He is coming; nay, he is here.

16

The Stewardship of the Supremacy of Christ

The men who have penned this book are outside the institutional church. Way outside. But we all keenly realize that just being outside the institutional church is no guarantee of a cure for anything.

The world abounds with tiny little groups that have come out of traditional churches, yet most of these groups seem to be going nowhere. Most have little purpose or focus, little or no revelation, little or no driving impetus.

In the light of this, we are forced to ask what was the secret of those rare groups such as the Waldensians, who lasted five hundred years! And in *all* those 500 years the Waldensians were red hot!! And in all those 500 years they never looked anything like the institutional church. The Waldensians held the torch in an age of an institutional church that was a *monolith*—a monolith that destroyed all competition and dissent. The institutional church marked the Waldensians for death . . . for 500 years.

Others who followed them, who meant business, were the United Brethren, the Moravians, the Plymouth Brethren, the Little Flock, the Bakht Singh movement of India. These are people who lived in contradiction to the practices of the established church *of their era.* In every case there is a calling, there is training, there is a commission, there is revelation, there is laying off the shackles of the prevailing mindset of *that* day. There is a gleam in the eye.

Now, contrast these great moves of God with all the purposeless little groups who exist today . . . groups that exist principally to comfort one another. Contrast these groups with the Waldensians, who were bent on revolt against the accepted, even at the cost of their lives. Dead set against the ordinary. Utterly opposed to the boring.

Such foundational revelation is rare! (And appears to be getting rarer?) A true *stewardship* of that revelation is even more rare!

Few outside the institutional church have a grasp of things unseen . . . of a stewardship of Christ's mystery. In the dearth of drought a thousand years old, nothing to give. Only an other-realm vision will deliver a people.

One more word. It has to do with Isaiah 61:4.

They shall rise up, they shall repair
the desolation of many generations.

What Isaiah speaks of here is a legitimate desire to have, but never is it to be the impetus, *never* must this be the driving force of a work! Christ is the driving force of God.

Someone once wisely said, "Only history will tell whether or not a particular people was a significant part of the witness to the Lord's Testimony."

With that in mind, in the next chapter we will take a look at matters virtually never considered, matters such as loss, such as failure. Things such as never getting big, always remaining small. Never being "successful," growing slowly, taking the long haul, and never being all that popular! That is, taking a full-faced look at hard reality.

17

Is the Church
an Organization, or . . . ?

It is given to those who lay a new foundation to also build. Those who build may never finish the task, still, they must build or die! They rarely are still alive when the fruit of their labors finally blossoms.

That which is built is *never* to be an organization.

You must not build an *organization*, for an organization is not of God. The church is an organism. *She* is an organism. She cannot be built, she can only be birthed. To build an organization and call it *God's* work is like calling a manufacturing plant a human being. That girl is a living organism. She is a she. You will hear that spoken as a platitude, but rarely will you see men willing to die for the reality of it. The point: You can create a vast organization with ease, and do it in one lifetime. To raise up a living organism . . . *that* is slow. And controversial, and unesteemed.

Even though the ekklesia *is* a living creature, still virtually all Christians build organizations. The building of an organization, with a Christian label, only tells us the organic expression of the assembly of God has been totally lost to the Christian mind. Men build . . . brick upon brick. A building that is alive is not built in this manner. We do not build *her* at all. Rather, the living stones grow! *They* form together.

She is not built structure upon structure, title upon title, office upon office, label upon label. Nor is she going through the motions of what is perceived to be *the organizational structure* of the New Testament church. There isn't such a thing in this girl. She is a lady, if you please.

No New Testament structure? There never has been. There never will be. This is a girl. Her biological genetics, her DNA, has been mistaken to be *New Testament structure*. No such structure exists in her. What you see in the New Testament is her DNA at work!

Not an organization? Is that possible? Not to the western mind, it is not. But to God, and to men of the first century, *yes*! And, by God's mercy, to a new breed of workers.

What you read in the New Testament is not the story of an organization. The New Testament does not give us a blueprint to glue together a church.

What you read in the New Testament is a girl growing into her natural expression. And *that* takes time.

You cannot organize an organic expression. You cannot call a girl into existence. That is a divine act. She *grows* up into a house, into a city, into a nation, and into a kingdom. Yet, in all this, she is *always* a *she*. She is not an *it*.

When you hear "what we need is the recovering of the gifts and offices of the first century" . . . head for the door. You are seeing the western mind about to create an organization. Organization is not the mind of God. God is far more simple than that. The "restoring" of teachers, evangelists, apostles, elders, or anything else does not bring forth the birth and growth of an organic woman. She comes forth biologically, as does any living creature. All else later emerges from out of her . . . naturally. And unfortunately for us Americans . . . *slowly*.

Can you see that the whole mindset of the institutional church must be laid aside? It thinks *organization*. It thinks fads. It holds out hope that tomorrow, for sure, things will change. It thinks clergy. It thinks "sit and listen" to sermons. It sees you as an audience, only an audience—a silent audience. You exist for the clergy; you are but instruments to further the work of the minister; that is all you are. It thinks laymen are not trustable to *be* the church. Clergy is *always* in charge; you always follow the clergy. It thinks ritual, form, program, Bible study classes, pulpit, and sermons. It thinks with the mind of Aristotle, not the mind of the other realm. Unfortunately, it also thinks that the present way of doing church *is* the way to have church.

If you are to see change—revolutionary change—you must abandon the present background. The institutional church and the institutional mind think *big*. God thinks small. True change, true restoration always begin small and begin slow. That is one of the reasons you almost never see professional ministers in the Lord's work outside the institutional church. Clergymen cannot stand small! Well, God works small. Let us continue to look at all these terrible attributes of God's work: small, slow, loss, failure, opposition, the long haul.

18

Women in Church Life

In virtually any church on earth women are second-class citizens. Sometimes it appears they are third-class citizens, literally oppressed. History shows that men oppress women, especially in religion. In the radical churches we live among, the women are *at least* our equals. We look to them to show us quite literally what church is. The ekklesia is a woman, and women must show us what that means.

You can tell when Christians leave the institutional church and start meeting informally. The first question asked is: "Should women be allowed to speak in the meeting?" Beware the legalist. He will insist women cannot. If his view prevails, there goes freedom . . . for everyone. And here comes second-class citizenship for women. The New Testament does *not* teach women are subordinate or silent in a gathering, nor second-class.

Until now, there has only been one group of Christians since the Reformation who gave full equality to women in the ekklesia. That is, the Quakers.

In virtually every church and denomination on this planet women are in some way second-class citizens.

Will this be true of the house church movement? Already a large segment of house church conferences across the English-speaking world teach that women should be silent in meetings and should cover their heads. There is also an inordinate emphasis on wives submitting to their husbands. The house church movement, in general, has resurrected an out-and-out erroneous interpretation of the Scripture. This is an old, well-worn path that we should never go down. If we go down this path . . . why bother . . . we have killed life even before life is born.

Take heart. In the radical house churches you will find women have equal standing with the men. It is not that they "are given an equal place"! No! It is not that they are given anything: It is their right to have equal standing. That equal standing cannot be taken away from them. In the church women decide for themselves what role they wish to play in the church.

As we men watch women find and take their place, we are a little awed by their capacities, gifts, insights and abilities!

This chapter makes no effort whatsoever to go into the intricacies of the erroneous teaching concerning a woman's place in the church. The brief sketch that follows is inadequate for a full grasp of this issue; nonetheless, here is a brief look at this subject.

Paul did not tell women what to wear on their heads. In I Corinthians Paul ends the section on head covering by making this very clear statement: "In the churches we have *no such* teaching." (I Corinthians, Chapter 11) Unfortunately, that statement has been translated to say, "We have no other teaching." This is an incorrect translation and every Bible scholar familiar with the Greek language knows that is an incorrect translation.

That ends the head covering issue.

What provoked this passage of Scripture in the first place? It was provoked by a furor that was going on in the ekklesia in Corinth. Why?

The *west* side of the city of Corinth were *Romans*. Roman women did *not* cover their heads for anything except when making offerings to heathen gods. (The men also covered their heads when making heathen sacrifices.)

The people who lived in the *center* of the city were *Greeks*. In their culture women who were married covered their heads. Women who were not married did not cover their heads.

On the *east* side of the city the people were from the Orient. *All* women from the Orient kept their heads covered.

This diversity, this clash of cultural practices, was causing problems in the Corinthian church. The Greeks were insisting that married women cover their heads. The people from the Orient were insisting that all women cover their heads. Roman women were saying, in effect, "Forget it, Roman women do not cover their heads!"

Corinth had a unique problem unknown to any other churches. It was a problem springing out of the fact that Corinth sat on an isthmus. Corinth had an Oriental part of its east side and a Roman part of its west side. Other Gentile churches never had any such problems. It was only the church in Corinth with its clashing cultures that was having this problem. This is why Paul said, "In the (other) churches we have no such teachings."

Sisters, be Romans.

Sisters, be free.

What about women speaking in a church gathering? Perhaps the greatest tragedy in this issue is the interpretation of Scripture which translates: "Women are not allowed to speak in the church." What that verse actually says is: "It is a shame for women to speak in the ekklesia." Paul tells the women not to speak in the ekklesia. The question is . . . what was the ekklesia?

The word *ekklesia* does not translate into the word *church*. It translates into the word *assembly*. Is this a reference to the assembly of Christ or the secular assembly of the city of Corinth? The local Corinthian government, the *secular* government, held an open ekklesia (assembly) in the marketplace from time to time. If a woman spoke out in such a gathering she was laughed at. If she was married, her husband was teased. Greeks were the most chauvinistic in all Europe. One book which traces the history of women in western Europe states that of all the nations in Europe the Greeks were the most extreme at keeping their women in subjugation.

Where does that leave you, the Christian woman?

Well, if you are ever in Greece, specifically in Corinth, and if there is a meeting of the entire city gathered in the marketplace, then your husband might well whisper to you, "Darling, please don't speak out while we are here in the marketplace. It will embarrass me!"

This was the custom in Corinth. (By the way, Corinth no longer exists!)

All of this has absolutely nothing to do with *the Lord's* assembly.

The ancient Greek assembly, held in the marketplace, has long passed away. Let not the ghost of an ancient secular assembly, where women did not speak, keep our women from speaking in the meetings of the house of God. We are not a secular assembly; we are *God's* assembly. The women speak in our meetings! (And remember, it is not that we men "let them speak." It is their right.)

And what of the passage in Ephesians that says women should submit themselves to their husbands? For hundreds of years this sentence has been preached with harshness and has opened the door to unbelievable abuse of womanhood.

It is better to emphasize the first part of that passage, which says: "Husbands love your wives." Also acknowledge another passage that says, in reference to men and women, "Submit you to one another."

This passage on submission has been so very, very abused. *And* it has been taken out of context. Women have been abused because ministers and Bible teachers proclaim that a woman should submit herself to her husband . . . without acknowledging the context of that passage. The context is *community*. The context is an *assembly*. An assembly in which everyone knows one another. This is the context! A church like that has checks and balances on a man's conduct.

On Sunday morning a couple walks into a church building and hears a preacher tell women to submit to their husbands. When the couple goes home there is no check and balance present. The husband yells at his wife. He threatens her with "the Word of

God says." In context, this passage penned by Paul had *checks and balances* built in. Unfortunately, *out of context* there is no protection. When taken out of context, this passage should *never* be applied. This passage was addressed to a people in church life. They lived in community. Today this context virtually does not exist. Therefore, until you find yourself in the context of this passage, then the passage is irrelevant. This passage was written for community and for people in community. Until a true community comes along—free of legalism, a community where women have their rightful place—until then, this passage only harms womanhood.

In the house churches we are in, if a man abused this passage in Ephesians, if he were not loving toward his wife, if he were threatening her with this passage on submission, he would hear from *all* the women in the church *and* all the men. That is the way it should be in proper community life. If a man were to treat his wife in such a degrading and denigrating way, the women in the church would be on his case; but the women would be in a race with the brothers in the church to see who got to this man first. Women are not mistreated in a healthy Christian community.

Repeat: The passage of Scripture is applicable only in its context. Paul was writing to a church. In that church everyone knew everyone. In that case the husband had better be loving his wife before any word of *submission* is ever uttered. I have never de-livered, nor heard, a message in our churches on women submitting; but I've heard a *great deal* about men loving their wives . . . delivered with the pas-sion, care and self-giving which Christ pours out on His bride. In community as it should be, you are never likely to see any abuse of a sister in Christ. It would not be tolerated for one instant. The women would make sure of that and so would the men.

Whatever else a person might believe about this subject, please remember that in Christ "there is no male or female."

In church life, that is, in Christian community, there should be, must be and *is* an incredible sense of freedom. For women. For men. For all. Beware of any church, in or out of the institutional system, that is otherwise.

And if all that you have read in this book seems implausible . . . then come and see!!

And be sure to talk to the women!

PART VI

The First Motion:

Restoring the Itinerant Worker

19

An Overview of the Worker

Most men who are leaders in typical house churches have very poor credentials to be leaders. Their credentials are mostly that they are dreamers, theorists, and philosophers. The typical worker, unfortunately, may have a good story, a great idea, or a fantastic vision (or is it a fantasy) of what a house church should be—but *no* credentials to show you when it comes to his training *in a house church*.

What do I mean by credentials? (1) Church life experience in a house church, (2) training under a man who is a church planter and who also has those same credentials, and (3) approval by his home church before ever having been sent out as a worker.

In the radical churches we see preparation as being long, thorough, and testing a man's mettle. Beyond that, his approval for entering the work rests with the church he is a member of.

First and foremost, the would-be worker should have *lived* in church life *before* ministry . . . before planting. It is a must to be in a house church before planting one. All other would-be workers are theorists, nothing more. They have no credentials! To follow one of these men is to follow an unknown, unbroken, inexperienced, self-orientated man. These are men who cannot say, "I lived in church life as an ordinary brother *before* I was approved by the church to go out and do the Lord's work."

Flee men who cannot give such a testimony. Generally speaking, those men cause more problems than they solve.

The world is full of such workers. Many are men obsessed with *preaching* . . . and preaching and preaching and preaching . . . and *ruling*. That is: *Their* house churches begin with *their* being the leader. Why bother going with such a man? You *already* had a clergyman! In fleeing this type of worker, you will also be fleeing the mess which he is about to create. (Note: If *his* house church fails, he will brush off his hands and, next year, he will start a movement to take Bibles to the South Pole, or some other Christian endeavor. The house church movement, for such men, is a suit to put on or take off as needed!) Not so the worker you need. He will live his whole life for the church.

Needed . . . firebrands! Firebrands born in the fire of the community of church life. Men who burn for, live for, and will gladly die for the planting of the body of Christ . . . the very bride of God's Son.

And one more thing, something really unprecedented: men who do not live off the gospel but who work for a living.

Do you have a worker? Or is there someone out there who is volunteering to be your worker? You might wish to ask him: "After you have been with us for a while, will you leave? Will you work toward *our* functioning and *your leaving?*"

Ask him to describe the house church (the not-in-the-institution church) he lived in as an ordinary brother before he started a house church. And ask him to tell you about the past history of churches outside the institutional church. Ask this: "Can you speak clearly of the Cathars, the Priscillianists, the Paulicans, the Waldensians, the United Brethren, the Celtic churches, the Moravians, the Plymouth Brethren, the Bogomils?" A worker outside the institutional church should be very conversant about these peoples.

(One man, when digging up everything he could on the Bogomils, soon exclaimed: "Why, they were heretics! They were Manichees! They were not even Christians." That is *not* digging up *facts;* that is digging up what the institutional church said about these people, things their *enemies* said about them.)

There was a price to be paid by all those who lived in days of yore who lit and carried the torch.

Anyone in history who took a stand outside the traditional church paid that price in blood.

It is no small thing when you hear it said, "We stand on the shoulders of giants." Part of a proper foundation for God's people—for workers, for a church that is revolutionary—is learning about what men of olden days did, what trials they passed through, what problems they faced, and how they resolved those problems.

There is homework to do, perhaps a lifetime of it, for any man who would be a worker outside institutional Christianity. "Has your would-be worker done his homework" *is* a pivotal question. If the answer is "no," then be assured there is no consuming fire in that man's bones!! Mark this: The men who followed Jesus Christ and stood before the Sanhedrin were illiterate! Nevertheless, they recounted the entire history of God's work. So also Stephen . . . so also Paul. In each case, those men *knew . . . the story.*

Knowing the past, and knowing it well, will produce a hunger, not born of ambition, to be a broken servant and to live a life that is stark reality. A hunger for spiritual depth! A *desperate* hunger to abandon one's background, to divest oneself of all the ways of institutional Christianity. A desperate leap to know and experience Christ in ways unknown to the traditional church. These are the elements which must be the hallmark of a new breed of worker.

If the house church movement is to turn the direction of Christian history and become the greatest factor ever in changing the practice of our faith, what else is needed?

First, revelation!

Startling, dramatic, and *new* revelation! Insight into God's ways, not familiar to today's generation. Things not seen, not heard, not experienced, not practiced, not known, nor dreamed in a dream ... things overlooked since Century One. Revelation from the Lord Jesus Christ and the Holy Spirit. This is something the Lord must give, for no man can give you revelation.

Men who will serve the Lord must not be driven by ambition, or be unbroken. These elements cannot be in men who are the pathfinders of radical revolution. To have something higher and purer, there must be a unique breed of men unknown in the past history of mainstream Christianity. This new breed will be the foundation layers of the future. These men *must* be driven by revelation.

Next, the ability to surrender *acceptance*. The "loss of the approval of man" is the greatest of all mountains this emerging worker must be endowed with to scale. Face the possibility of losing all acceptance ... because you departed from accepted ways.

That which is accepted is not always correct.

That which is correct is not always accepted.

To misquote Shakespeare: "To live, to run, to succeed or fail, and then to die outside the acceptance of traditional Christianity, ah, there is the rub."

But take comfort in this: If you know the long, beautiful, though bloody, story of Christians who have dared live outside the traditionally accepted practices of Christianity which existed in their day, you will find comfort in knowing that while you may not be accepted in traditional Christianity, you are within the bounds of *historic* Christianity!

To my brothers in the house church movement I plead: Move in this direction and you *will* lose your acceptance, your reputation. You will gain only ignominy. But climb that mountain, and you will be a man among men.

What else is needed? The foundation for a new work of God must *not* have as its rallying cry, "We must get back to the Bible! Study the Bible! Master the Bible!"

If you make this mantra the drive of any new work, you are in reverse gear. You are going back to ways that are old, yes, but they are *not* old enough. For centuries, "Study your Bible" has been the rally cry of all new works. In the light of the little that has resulted from "Study your Bible," the only conclusion we can reach is that for hundreds of years we must not have studied the Bible hard enough, read it long enough, or applied it thoroughly enough. Surely someone *did* read the Bible long enough, well enough, thoroughly enough. Still, in the 200 years in which western Europe and America have been fervently studying the Bible, it has not set off a single revolution.

Many men *have* mastered the Bible, and absolutely *nothing revolutionary* has come out of it. There are millions of Bible classes, as well as thousands of Bible schools, all over this planet . . . and so it has been for nearly two centuries; yet Christianity has remained shallow. There must be some missing ingredient to this back-to-the-Bible rallying call. Dare we say this sacred mantra is lacking something?!

It is time we get to the *real*, overlooked, foundation! How about *this* for our foundation: Jesus, the Christ!

Bible study has not lived up to its billing. It needs an added ingredient—Christ!

And . . . *the church*!!

If ever we are to see any major change, then the centrality of Jesus Christ must be there—and not only present, but the centrality of Christ . . . *experienced*.

The idea of "mastering the Bible as the secret to the Christian life" is actually an old and worn-out concept which did not prove to live up to what it was advertised to do back in 1820 when this statement first took root and it does not today.

So also tongues, when this first began to be popularized back in the 1920's. So also submission, so also covering, so also miracles, so also prophecy, so also the gifts, so also "the five-fold ministries," so also renewal, so also worship, so also power, so also revival, so also "preach the Word." All these elements were presented to us as *the* lost secret which would change everything; yet none have produced the lasting change they were advertised to accomplish. Most "renewals" of each of these ingredients turned out to be warmed-over fads that waned within a matter of a few years. These things which have over and over been presented to us as *the* solution have failed because they are all encased in crinkled, inelastic, shriveled, worn-out old wineskins. What is that wineskin? A dead way of doing Sunday morning church! *That* worn-out old wineskin. And a typical run-of-the-mill house church is not a new wineskin, nor does it have new wine!

Let's make a confession: (1) We have studied the Bible, and the old wine and the old wineskin never moved. (2) Nobody has dared to challenge the *wineskin* and said "This isn't scriptural, it is dead, and it has to go. (3) Even though we have *studied* the New

Testament, we have not *experienced the Christ of the New Testament.*

This new emerging worker dares challenge the old wineskin and he introduces a new wine. It is Christ. And the new kind of wineskin is a return to the ancient practice of church. Does this man also honor the Bible? Read it? Study it? Teach it? Well, ask him! And ask him questions concerning the New Testament. He may blow your mind with his answers. He may just prove to be very well grounded in the New Testament. But you will never otherwise know that fact because he is too busy pointing you to Christ!

Abandoning *all* present-day practices, heading straight for Christ and His ekklesia, reintroducing the ekklesia as she was long ago, these have not yet been tried!

Whatever is part of this foundation must be revolutionary, new, unique, and experience-able. That is, it can be *experienced,* not just talked about. Such sacred ways are unknown to the last thousand years of Christianity.

The wind, the fire, the light and the storm come from new, powerful, overwhelming, transforming *revelation* given by the Holy Spirit. Christ and the ekklesia are not fads. These are not doctrines, nor ideas, nor teachings. These are floods of consuming fire—new, fresh revelation of Jesus Christ and Him alone.

And with that revelation, *practical handles* are needed as to the "how" of knowing Him intimately. This revelation and this revolution will not be a series of messages. It will be an overwhelming impact of personal encounter with the Lord Jesus Christ; and it will be, from top to bottom, a whole new practice of the ekklesia. Brass tack, bedrock practicality. Add to that a daily experience of Christ *in the ekklesia.*

If you are to be a worker, you must have revelation of Christ that is new, fresh. Encountering Christ, *knowing* Him, is not and must not be only the experience of the worker. The ways of knowing Christ are simple enough, practical enough, that the most ordinary brother or sister can grasp and experience Him; and the worker must see to it that an environment is created where the emphasis is on getting to know Christ. The worker must be capable of showing God's people, in the simplest of terms, the "how" of getting to know Christ.

The foundation was Christ, is Christ, and must always be Christ. There is *no other* foundation.

Be advised: There are eighteen hundred years worth of rubble that must be cleared away in order to lay so new and radical a foundation. It is a gigantic leap *forward* to *return* to first-century ways.

Those who claim to have the calling and the commission to see the church rebuilt must have the foundational truth of God's house revealed to them. *And* they must have lived in, known and experienced the house of God before attempting to draw others into that building experience.

All this calls for a wholly different species of worker. Only such unusual men will lay this unique foundation.

Why does nothing in the institutional church ever *really* change? Why does the same cookie-cutter minister keep emerging, generation after generation!

20

You Wish to Be a Worker?

If you think God does not start with the small, then remember He started the whole process of humanity with one man and one woman! That day God showed He was not a God who was in a rush!

The Father took an eternity to train His Son before sending Him to earth. Then He added thirty years of training *on* earth. The result of this slow, small beginning? God got *one man*! God is slow when it comes to *His* work.

Just *one* man! Beyond that, *twelve* men. It was twelve men staying, and staying in just one city. Twelve men in one city . . . and only one church on this planet, for years. (They were stuck in Jordan, while the rest of the world was lost in sin.)

Secondly, God begins a great thing in a small way, and He begins it with a despised man and a despised people.

Do not walk this way if you are a little uncomfortable at being classified with Bogomils,

Waldensians, Albigensians, Priscillianists, Lollards and Anabaptists.

Today's mindset would have seen to it that the human race started with a hundred thousand people, so that things could move along quickly. When God decided to come to earth He started with a young girl. (The girl was accused of being adulterous because she was not married when she became pregnant.)

God started in a small way, with a despised girl.

That rumor about His mother and His legitimacy hung over the head of Jesus Christ all His life. A despised man with a despised mother.

Look at history. God's men are almost always born in a barn, or the likes of a barn, usually a hillbilly from the country. Almost never has God used a city slicker. Yes, there are exceptions, but the exceptions are rare.

What of Paul!

Paul personally raised up no more than perhaps thirteen churches in his lifetime. *All* of these beginnings of all these churches were small. Also, these churches were delicate and filled with great problems, *daily*. The churches Paul raised up were all filled with set-backs, failure, criticism and rejection.

Now, to you! Do you feel that raising up a *prevailing* house church is a cakewalk? Know this: The institutional church knows *nothing* of the problems of people being thrown together. And until you are thrown together with a group of Christians, you cannot imagine the difficulties which arise. The birth of a church is *never* a cakewalk.

Potentially, a house church has a hundred times more problems than an institutional church. It is because we are fallen, and that fact shows up, larger and more realistic, when you really know the people you meet with.

Now take a deep breath as we move to the very heart and soul of failure, loss, small, and slow. Now see that the word despised does not fall just on Jesus and His mother. It falls on all who dare to not conform to the system of their day.

You wish to be part of a revolution, maybe even a *worker* in that revolution? Then consider the following price.

21

The High Cost of Torch Bearing

We all honor David the king. But there was a time in his life when no one would have thought of him as a great man. Virtually everyone in Israel and the surrounding countries despised him. His name was a parable to frighten children. Therefore note this:

God always begins with *despised* men.

If any part of the house church is to succeed, if any part of it is to emerge to revolutionize the entire landscape of Christianity, it will surely require that *new breed of worker* of which we have spoken and a daring group of people. Neither of them will ever make the "most popular list."

Answer this, you who would serve in the vineyard of God: Are you willing to be a simple, *ordinary* brother in community, in church life? Are you willing to enter the rugged reality of knowing life together with others—at close range?

How well do you know church life and house church living? Maybe this is the same question, but stated in a more dramatic fashion: How well do you know the cross?

(By the way if you ask a house church leader these questions. . . and if he stutters . . . *run!*)

Next, ask yourself: Can I be despised, yet never bitter? Can I blast away the rubble, then with pure words and pure heart, without a single negative sentence, turn and give Christ and Christ alone in ministry to God's people? Only broken men do such things.

Those who dare to follow a man who is truly prepared to serve in *this* vineyard will not follow that man because he is acceptable. They follow him because something within them has a knowing. They follow him when he is not King David. There is no crown on his head. He is an unknown, unheard of. And those who have heard of him despise him.

Such are the days of foundation laying!

There *is* a *torch*, there is a testimony, there are those who have been stewards of that torch and that testimony throughout all these last 1800 years. Such peoples always existed, but they were small. And they were despised!

Small and despised does not easily fit the mind of our generation. Add to that the high possibility of failure.

Ask about how, in every case, their witness eventually flickered and died. For a breathless moment the torch hung suspended. At that breathless moment, some foolhardy soul—some small, despised man or people who had a revelation of Jesus Christ—grasped the torch again, held it high and moved it yet higher up.

Once more the light flares bright. The testimony lives.

Whither the house church movement?!

22

Scripture Reveals
the Itinerant Worker

How were the ekklesias in the first century *raised up*? Virtually every church in the first century was birthed at the hands of an extra-local, itinerant (traveling) worker. This person is known by the following names: "apostle," "sent one," "worker," "foundation layer," "church planter," et al. (The few churches mentioned in the New Testament that emerged without the direct aid of an itinerant worker were always helped by such a worker after its birth.)

How does God produce such workers?

Workers emerge from the soil of an existing ekklesia. Such a worker is one who has been called, trained, and sent by God to birth ekklesias. He is someone who has been given a unique revelation of Christ and His eternal purpose. He is someone who is well acquainted with *the mystery*. And he has been specially equipped by God to unveil that mystery to others.

For this reason, a large part of a worker's preparation for service is to live in the context of an already existing ekklesia before he is sent out. It is there that he both experiences and learns the spiritual and practical realities of the Divine mystery.

This process of training was true of all the itinerant workers mentioned in the New Testament. First-century workers did not leave the synagogue on Saturday and decide to plant churches on Sunday! They first experienced that which they were sent out to plant. This principle is most critical. Aspiring "church planters" who have never lived a day in the context of a first-century style ekklesia should take serious heed to this principle.

A seminary education cannot equip a person to raise up the ekklesia—nor can any position in an institutional church! Only time spent in a living, breathing, vital expression of the body of Christ (without an organizational hierarchy) can equip one for such work.

To frame it another way, you cannot produce that which you have never experienced! What is more, the gore and glory, the testing and transforming, the sifting and soaring, the brokenness and beautifying, the exposure and enlargement that body life affords is absolutely vital for preparing those who are called to God's work.

To blithely launch out to plant a house church without such preparation is sheer presumption. It reflects a misunderstanding of God's ways. The exacting nature of the ekklesia is designed to prevent would-be workers from becoming clergy-on-wheels who lord over local churches like distant bosses. Living in ekklesia life as a non-leader fosters brokenness and humility. Living in church life for a long time makes a worker safe to God's people. Further, if a man ventures out to start a house church without such preparation, that church will invariably fall on its face.

23

A Consistent Pattern

We are itinerant men. We *leave* the churches we raise up . . . and—from that moment—God's people run the church. We return from time to time to strengthen and encourage. We also show up if—and only if—there is a desperate crisis in that church.

Are we on good scriptural ground? Yes. The best of scriptural grounds. In fact the *only* scriptural grounds!

The principle of the itinerant worker and his preparation can be consistently traced throughout the entire New Testament story. Here is a brief synopsis:

Jesus Christ

Jesus Christ lived in the corporate experience of the Godhead while He was on earth (Col. 2:9). He was called, trained, and sent by His Father to be the first apostolic worker (John 4:34; 9:4; Heb. 3:1; Matt. 16:18). For three years the Lord Jesus planted the embryo of the ekklesia in the hearts of the twelve disciples as they lived in community under His direct Headship (Matt. 3:13-14).

The Twelve

The twelve lived in the corporate experience of Christ for three years. They were called, trained, and sent by Jesus Christ (John 17:18). Afterwards, the twelve planted the first church in the city of Jerusalem (Acts 2-6). Under persecution the Jerusalem church dispersed and was transplanted all over Palestine (Acts 8:1-4; 9:31). These twelve men itinerantly visited the newly transplanted churches. They laid fresh foundations of Christ among those new churches (Acts 8-12).

Barnabas

After the twelve, we see a man named Barnabas in this same pattern. Barnabas lived in the corporate experience of the church in Jerusalem for at least twelve years. Barnabas was called by God, trained and sent by the twelve (Acts 4:36-37; 9:27; 11:22). Afterwards, he laid a foundation of *Christ* in the church of Antioch, Syria (Acts 11:23,26).

Paul

Paul lived in the corporate experience of the church in Antioch for at least five years. Paul was called by God and trained by Barnabas, who was trained by the twelve (Acts 11:25-26,30; 12:25). Afterwards, Paul and Barnabas were sent by the Holy

Spirit to the work of planting churches in heathen lands (Acts 13:1-4). Paul and Barnabas planted four churches in the region of South Galatia: Pisidian Antioch, Iconium, Lystra, and Derbe (Acts 13-14).

Silas

Silas lived in the corporate experience of the church in Jerusalem for at least fifteen years. Silas was called by God and trained by the twelve in Jerusalem (Acts 15:22,27,32). Afterwards, Paul and Silas were sent out by the church in Antioch. The two men went forth and planted four churches in Greece: Philippi, Thessalonica, Berea, and Corinth (Acts 15:40-18:21).

Paul's Eight Co-Workers

In Ephesus, Paul trained and sent eight men to plant churches in Asia Minor. Before they were trained, before they were sent, all of these men previously lived in the corporate experience of the churches where they originated: Titus was from Antioch; Timothy was from Lystra; Gaius was from Derbe; Aristarchus and Secundus were from Thessalonica; Sopater was from Berea; Tychicus and Trophimus were from Ephesus (Acts 20:4). Among the churches these men planted were Thyatira, Philadelphia, Smyrna, Pergamum, and Sardis (Acts 19:10; Rev. 2-3).

Epaphras

Epaphras appears to have lived in the corporate experience of the church in Ephesus while Paul was ministering there. Epaphras was called by God, trained, and sent by the Holy Spirit to co-work with Paul (Col. 1:7). Afterwards, Epaphras planted three churches in the Lycus valley: Colossae, Laodicea, and Hierapolis (Col. 1:2,6-7; 4:12-13).

So the Scriptures are clear. Virtually all workers in the first-century were first called and subsequently trained in the context of ekklesia life. This means that they lived in the ekklesia as brothers, not as leaders. Only after this training were they sent into the work of planting churches.

And they *traveled*. They *never* settled in one place. They helped churches, but did not stay to become a resident *priest*.

Repeat: In all of the above cases, the workers never resided in the churches they planted. After they laid foundations and equipped the local saints to minister Christ to one another, they *left* the churches to the Holy Spirit. (In the case of the persecution in Jerusalem, the church left the apostles!) The workers would then periodically return to the churches to strengthen and encourage them, but they would always leave again. Theirs was truly an itinerant ministry.

24

Whither the House
Church Movement?

The divine principle of extra-local, itinerant worker is the forgotten chapter in the first-century story. It is the overlooked pattern of the first-century church. It is the neglected ministry in the body of Christ. And yet there is far more Biblical currency for this pattern than there is for home meetings, plural elders, open-participatory gatherings, and every other practice that those who meet in homes arduously defend by quoting chapter and verse out of the New Testament.

To see a richer expression of the body of Christ we will return to these first principles of God's work. Otherwise, things will go on the way they are now, and God's timeless purpose will wait in the wings for another generation. And the house church movement will be nothing more than bands of Christians leaving the organized church, assembling in homes, and conversing over java and cookies. This is not who I am, nor is this what the other men are who penned this book. We labor in the majestic, unfathomable, eternal purpose to which God has called His people: Jesus Christ, in all His fullness, visible on this planet. We live in a world, albeit a small one, where God's people become experientially one with Him.

In light of the staggering nature of the divine intention, the only answer is men called by God to raise up the Lord's house. Broken and tested men who have lived in ekklesia life. Men who have a deep and living knowledge of Jesus Christ. Men who have profound insight into the mystery of God. Men who can impart this revelation into others with vision and power.

The need of the hour is for such men to wait on God until they are trained and sent. Men who, once sent, will plant the ekklesia in the same way that first-century workers did: by equipping the people in the ekklesia, then abandoning that people to the Holy Spirit! Equally needed is for the body of Christ to recognize the role of such men. May the scores of Christians who are even now leaving institutional Christianity see their need for itinerant workers (1 Cor. 12:18-21,28; Eph. 4:7-16).

AN APPEAL

Today is a day of restoration. It is also a day of repairing. Repairing the corporate testimony of God's people is no small thing. While there is no shortage of Christians in America, there is a mammoth dearth of corporate testimony. God's foremost desire is to secure a people in every locale that are foundationally constituted and built together as a visible, locatable, geographical, corporate expression of His Son (Col. 2:2,19; Eph. 2:21-22; 4:16; 1 Pet. 2:5).

Christians who have left the institutional church, no matter how long they have been saved, will have an awfully hard time going on with other Christians in a face-to-face community which has no human headship. Thus a worker who knows the headship of Christ—who has experienced genuine ekklesia life with all of its glory and gore and who has been broken by the cross—is an indispensable resource for helping believers discover how to gather under Christ's headship.

We are here for His highest. We mean to plant the flag of that testimony on heights of ground not trodden since the days of the founders of the faith.

And you?

WE HAVE LIVED THAT
WHICH WE HAVE WRITTEN

You have heard us say that meetings sometimes last three and four hours and still no one wants to go home. We have been in such meetings.

We have said freedom abounds in these churches. We are children of that freedom.

We have said there is no legalism in these churches. We have lived in the pure glory of that fact.

We have said "come visit." Once each of us came and visited.

We have said to men and women who desire to be workers: Come, be a brother, an ordinary brother, in the brotherhood. Let the church get to know you . . . as a layman who works for a living. Be sure that we have sat, as brothers in the church and in brothers meetings . . . and been ordinary men who earn our living.

We have said we have been trained in the church. We have also been trained by an old man, outside the institutional church, who has spent thirty years planting churches. That old man, in turn, once sat as a brother in church life . . . earning his own living . . . before he raised up a church. He is also itinerant. We are itinerant.

We have stated that living in community is not easy. Not at first. And that it is exposing. But it is also the greatest, most wonderful experience of life.

We have said you may know Christ in the depths. We have walked in those depths.

We have said there can be meetings in which Jesus Christ—Christ *experienced*—is the only topic of the meetings. We have been—and *are*—in those meetings.

We have spoken of now living in an expression of the church that is unlike anything on this earth—totally different, from top to bottom. We are in that revolution.

We have said that women are free and equal. Come ask them!

We have not written one sentence of theory in this book. We have lived everything we have stated.

Come and see.

Oh, by the way, when we get old, we have it in our hearts to train men and women the way in which we have been trained.

If you feel you belong in this revolution, then come and see. Then if your heart sings to this anthem, come and stay!

THE AUTHORS

All the men who penned this book (1) plant churches and (2) work for a living. All are itinerant. All lived in church life before being involved in their present ministries.

Tom Begier is an electronic specialist. Tim Richey's occupation has been that of a haberdasher for virtually his entire adult life. Both Nick Vasiliades and Frank Viola are school teachers.

All can be reached by writing SeedSowers Publishing House.

THE CALF-PATH

One day, through the primeval wood,
A calf walked home, as good calves should;
But made a trail all bent askew,
A crooked trail as all calves do.

Since then two hundred years have fled,
And, I infer, the calf is dead.
But still he left behind his trail,
And thereby hangs my moral tale.

The trail was taken up next day
By a lone dog that passed that way;
And then a wise bell-wether sheep
Pursued the trail o'er vale and steep,
And drew the flock behind him, too,
As good bell-wethers always do.

And from that day, o'er hill and glade,
Through those old woods a path was made;
And many men wound in and out,
And dodged, and turned, and bent about
And uttered words of righteous wrath
Because 'twas such a crooked path.

But still they followed—do not laugh—
The first migrations of that calf,
And through this winding wood-way stalked
Because he wobbled when he walked.

This forest path became a lane,
That bent, and turned, and turned again;
This crooked lane became a road,
Where many a poor horse with his load
Toiled on beneath the burning sun,
And traveled some three miles in one.
And thus a century and a half
They trod the footsteps of that calf.

The years passed on in swiftness fleet,
The road became a village street;
And this, before men were aware,
A city's crowded thoroughfare;
And soon the central street was this
Of a renowned metropolis;
And men two centuries and a half
Trod in the footsteps of that calf.

Each day a hundred thousand rout
Followed the zigzag calf about;
And o'er his crooked journey went
The traffic of a continent.

A hundred thousand men were led
By one calf near three centuries dead.
They followed still his crooked way,
And lost one hundred years a day;
For thus such reverence is lent
To well-established precedent.

A moral lesson this might teach,
Were I ordained and called to preach;
For men are prone to go it blind
Along the calf-paths of the mind,
And work away from sun to sun
To do what other men have done.
They follow in the beaten track,
And out and in, and forth and back,
And still their devious course pursue,
To keep the path that others do.

But how the wise old wood-gods laugh,
Who saw the first primeval calf!
Ah! Many things this tale might teach—
But I am not ordained to preach.

Sam Walter Foss

SeedSowers

THE WORKS OF T. AUSTIN-SPARKS

The Centrality of Jesus Christ...19.95
The House of God...29.95
Ministry..29.95
Service..19.95

COMFORT AND HEALING

A Tale of Three Kings *(Edwards)*...8.95
The Prisoner in the Third Cell *(Edwards)*............................5.95
Letters to a Devastated Christian *(Edwards)*........................5.95
Healing for those who have been Crucified by Christians *(Edwards)*.........8.95
Dear Lillian *(Edwards)*..5.95

OTHER BOOKS ON CHURCH LIFE

Climb the Highest Mountain *(Edwards)*...............................9.95
The Torch of the Testimony *(Kennedy)*................................14.95
The Passing of the Torch *(Chen)*..9.95
Going to Church in the First Century *(Banks)*......................5.95
When the Church was Young *(Loosley)*.................................14.95
Church Unity *(Litzman, Nee, Edwards)*.................................14.95
Let's Return to Christian Unity *(Kurosaki)*...........................14.95

CHRISTIAN LIVING

Final Steps in Christian Maturity *(Guyon)*..........................12.95
Turkeys and Eagles *(Lord)*..8.95
Beholding and Becoming *(Coulter)*......................................8.95
Life's Ultimate Privilege *(Fromke)*.......................................7.00
Unto Full Stature *(Fromke)*...7.00
All and Only *(Kilpatrick)*...7.95
Adoration *(Kilpatrick)* 8.95
Release of the Spirit *(Nee)* 5.00
Bone of His Bone *(Huegel)* 8.95
Christ as All in All *(Haller)* 9.95

Please write or call for our current catalog:

SeedSowers
P.O. Box 3317
Jacksonville, FL 32206
800-228-2665
(800-ACT-BOOK)
Fax: 904-598-3456
www.seedsowers.com

Books you might like to read

◆ Radical books for radical readers

BEYOND RADICAL

A simple, historical introduction into how we got all of our present-day Christian practices.

You will be thunderstruck to discover that there is really *nothing* we are doing today in our church practice that came directly out of man's determination to be scriptural. Virtually everything we do came into being sometime during church history, after the New Testament. We have spent the rest of our time trying to bend the Scripture to justify the practice.

WHEN THE CHURCH WAS LED *ONLY* BY LAYMEN

The word *elder* appears in the New Testament seventeen times, the word *pastor* appears only once (and nobody knows what that word had reference to, because there is no place in the first-century story in which he is clearly seen).

But there are over one hundred and thirty references from the day of Pentecost forward that refer to either "brothers" or "brothers and the sisters" (Greek: *Adolphus*). *These* were the people who were leading the church. There are only two major players, from a human viewpoint, upon the first-century stage. They are the church planters and God's people—the brothers and the sisters. Everything else is a footnote.

OVERLOOKED CHRISTIANITY

What is the view of the Trinity on these three critical aspects of faith:

1. How to live the Christian life
2. What is "church" really supposed to look like
3. How are workers—specifically *church* planters—supposed to be trained

Revolutionary, radical and arresting! These are the words which best describe this one-of-a-kind book!

Overlooked Christianity makes a great companion book to *Rethinking Elders* and gives clear answers about *what to do* in the practice of our Christian life!

AN OPEN LETTER TO
HOUSE CHURCH LEADERS

A simple statement on what a more primitive expression of the Christian faith should be centering on.

◆ Books which show what the Christian faith was like "first-century style"

REVOLUTION, the Story of the Early Church
THE SILAS DIARY
THE TITUS DIARY
THE TIMOTHY DIARY
PRISCILLA'S DIARY
THE GAIUS DIARY

The story! Perhaps the best way we will ever understand what it was like from the day of Pentecost in 30 A.D. until the close of the first century is simply to know the story. Allow yourself to be treated to, and enthralled by, that story. (Warning: Knowing the story will change your life forever.) You will find that story in every detail, with nothing missing, in these *six* books.

◆ Books which glorify Jesus Christ

THE DIVINE ROMANCE
A book of awe, wonder and beauty.

THE STORY OF MY LIFE AS TOLD BY JESUS CHRIST
Matthew, Mark, Luke and John combined into one complete gospel written in first-person singular.

ACTS IN FIRST-PERSON
Beginning with Acts 1, Peter tells the story of Acts through chapter 11. Then Barnabas, speaking in first person, tells the story of Acts from chapter 13 to chapter 15. You then hear Silas, Timothy and Luke continue the story all the way through, ending with chapter 28.

THE CHRONICLES OF THE DOOR
The record of heaven as told in;
THE BEGINNING
THE ESCAPE
THE BIRTH
THE TRIUMPH
(the resurrection)
THE RETURN

◆ Books which show you how to experience Christ

The following books serve as an introduction to the Deeper Christian Life:
LIVING BY THE HIGHEST LIFE
THE SECRET TO THE CHRISTIAN LIFE
THE INWARD JOURNEY

◆ Books that heal

Here are books that have been used all over the world, and in many languages, to heal Christians from the deep, deep pains they experience as they go through life. Some were written for Christians who have been damaged by their churches and damaged by other Christians. Others are books which help you understand the ways of God as they are now working in your life. All of these books are known and loved around the world.

A TALE OF THREE KINGS

A study in brokenness based on the story of Saul, David and Absalom.

THE PRISONER IN THE THIRD CELL

A study in the mysteries of God's ways, especially when He works contrary to all your understanding and expectations of Him.

CRUCIFIED BY CHRISTIANS

Healing for Christians who have been crucified by other Christians.

LETTERS TO A DEVASTATED CHRISTIAN

This book explores different techniques practiced by Christian groups who demand extreme submission and passivity from their members. It faces the difficult task of dealing with bitterness and resentment and rebuilding of faith and trust.

Contact SeedSowers Publishing House for a catalog of these and other books, including great classics from the past on the deeper Christian life, as well as new publications that will be appearing annually.

SeedSowers
PO Box 3317
Jacksonville, FL32206
800-228-2665
www.seedsowers.com